A HUNDRED
YEARS A-GROWING

First published in 2010 by
Liberties Press
Guinness Enterprise Centre | Taylor's Lane | Dublin 8
www.libertiespress.com | info@libertiespress.com
+353 (1) 415 1287

Trade enquiries to CMD BookSource
55a Spruce Avenue | Stillorgan Industrial Park
Blackrock | County Dublin
tel: +353 (1) 294 2560 | Fax: +353 (1) 294 2564

Distributed in the United States by
Dufour Editions
PO Box 7 | Chester Springs | Pennsylvania | 19425

and in Australia by
James Bennett Pty Limited | InBooks
3 Narabang Way | Belrose NSW 2085

Copyright © Gillian Finan, 2010

The author has asserted her moral rights.
ISBN: 978-1-907593-06-2

2 4 6 8 10 9 7 5 3 1
A CIP record for this title is available from the British Library.

Typeset in Agaramond by Sin É Design
Printed by Printware

A HUNDRED
YEARS A-GROWING

A HISTORY OF THE
IRISH GIRL GUIDES

GILLIAN FINAN

CONTENTS

Previous: *The Irish Harp being played at Pax Ting in 1939.*

Overleaf: *Camp Conway participants 1923.*

For all the women who inspire us

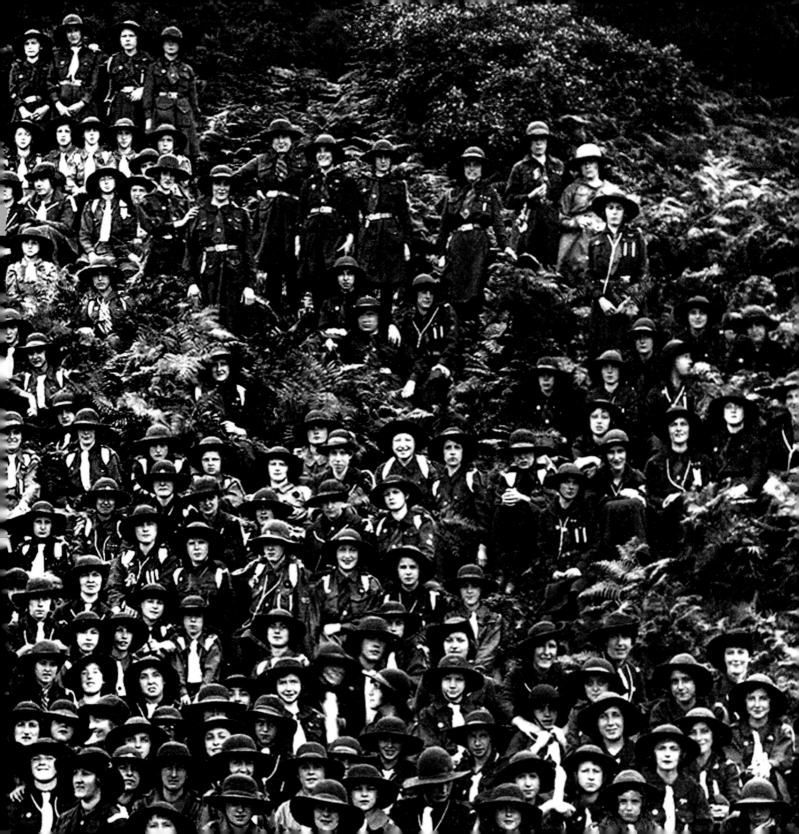

BE PREPARED

This is to Certify that

The Fourth Dublin

Company of B.P. Girl Guides

is duly registered at Headquarters

Signed

Agnes Baden-Powell   President

Date January 1ᵉ 1916

ACKNOWLEDGEMENTS

When I agreed to write this book for the Irish Girl Guides, I never imagined how it would consume me and take over my life. I also never realised how much support and help I would need. There are so many people I need to thank.

To Barry I owe the greatest debt. He has always supported me in all my endeavours and nothing ever left my desk without him reading it first. Without his unfailing love and support none of this would have been possible.

To my family – Dermot, Catherine, Damian and Granny Davis – thank you for the love and support, which I could always take for granted. To my next-door neighbours John and Frances O'Connor, who are a second set of parents, as they already know.

A special thank-you must go to those who read and edited the book. Firstly, to Seán O'Keeffe from Liberties, whose patience and guidance over the past few months have been invaluable. Also, to Jenny Gannon, who read every word and whose advice was both insightful and incredibly useful.

Thank you to all in the Irish Girl Guides who supported and advised me throughout the process. In particular the head of our Centenary celebrations, Diane Dixon, who was always on hand to read, advise and find photos. A special thank-you goes to the IGG Archive Group – Margaret Dunne, Hazel Convery, Dorothy O'Ferrall and Hannah Keating – who worked tirelessly rooting out photos, reading the text and finding any additional information I needed. To our CEO, Linda Peters, who allowed me to camp in National Office while I

Registration Certificate of the 4th Dublin Company 1916.

accessed the archives and Maeve O'Reilly who searched high and low in National Office for long-lost and forgotten photos: thank you Maeve.

My most sincere thanks goes to Jenny Gannon and Lorna Finnegan, who gave up an entire bank-holiday weekend to edit upwards of 250 photos – and thank you Jenny for feeding us. I couldn't have done it without them.

Thank you to everyone who was interviewed or contributed quotes, thoughts, or photos to the book. In particular Ollie Ballantine, Patricia Boate, Sarah Browne, Gill Buckley, Colleen Clarke, Joy Clarke, Lua Clarke, Mary Clarke, Helen Concannon, Lisa Concannon, Margaret Corr, Karina Dingerkus, Diane Dixon, Alex Findlater, Lorna Finnegan, Jenny Gannon, Jenna Goodwin, Emma Harvey, Elspeth Henderson, Rose Hennessy, Deirdre Henley, Ruth Hughes, Vanessa Wyse Jackson, Jill Kavanagh, Freda Keady, Maria Kidney, Nicola Le Roux, Tamsin Le Roux, Jemma Lee, Hazel Murphy, Elaine O'Connell, Catherine O'Connor, Rosemary O'Driscoll, Amanda O'Sullivan, Paul O'Sullivan, Emer O'Sullivan, Máire McInerney, Marg McInerney, Margaret McKenna, Lisa Finan McSweeney, Irene Reale, Katherine Ryan, Karen Stapley, Vivian Pigott, Fióna Walsh, Sr. Anne Patrick Walshe and Violet Warner. In particular, thank you to *Girlguiding UK*, the *Irish Times*, the *Irish Examiner* and the *National Archives of Ireland*.

This project definitely could not have been completed without my friends, who provided just the right levels of emotional and practical support: Sheila Booth, Eimear Cruise, Emma Proctor Dickinson, Aoife Duignan, Mark Duncan, Sinead Egan, Lorna Finnegan, Pamela Fraher, Jenny Gannon, Carole Holohan (for selflessly volunteering her thesis), Eoin Kinsella, Ann Marie Long, Kelley Maxham, Ciara Meehan, Maren Muckler, Kate Mulligan, Eilis O'Leary, Amanda O'Sullivan and Paul Rouse. A special thanks to Elizabeth Dawson and Fióna

Walsh for all the dinners, and a place to lay my head after a long day.

Thanks to Phil, Paddy and Sean Whyte for their support and interest in my work.

Although in preparing this work I spoke or corresponded with a number of people, all errors remain my own.``

FOREWORD

Opposite: *Lady Powerscourt presenting the Ross Cup.*

As we reach the centenary of Guiding in Ireland, it's time to celebrate and to document the history of our organisation. Guiding began in Ireland in 1911 and although it has evolved since then, the core values of Guiding have remained throughout. Our Promise and Law lay down for us the basis of what we do. This is practically the same Promise and Law used by the 10 million members of Guiding worldwide. It is what links us to each other and to members worldwide. Our programmes have developed and changed over time, however, as our society and the needs of our members have changed. For instance, today, rather than doing a signalling or cobbling badge, the girls can do badges in areas such as voting, drugs awareness, renewable energy and computer skills.

Guiding allows girls and young women to develop to their fullest potential as responsible citizens of the world. We do this in a non-formal educational environment and depend so much on our volunteer leaders. Our members range from five-year-old Ladybirds to our adult leaders. Throughout our programmes, we help the girls to think for themselves and to be self-sufficient team leaders and team players.

We do not have documentary evidence as to how many girls and women have been members of the Irish Girl Guides. While many have been involved for only a few years, others have had a lifelong involvement in the movement. As girls and new adult members, we feel part of a local organisation. As our time in Guiding develops, this feeling relates also to the national organisation, and further growth brings us to the realisation that we belong locally, nationally and internationally all at the same time. This book will provide you with a snapshot of our achievements and memories over the last hundred years. I would like to say thanks to Gillian for taking the time to write this book, and to the members of the Archives Team and Diane Dixon as chairman of our centenary committee for their input, time and effort in getting this publication to print.

I think we should all be proud of the Irish Girl Guides as we celebrate a centenary of Guiding, and I look forward to leading the IGG into our second century.

Emer O'Sullivan
Chief Commissioner
Irish Girl Guides

Cadets marching at a rally in Iveagh Gardens in 1948.

CHAPTER 1

The Beginnings of the Girl Guide Movement

T he dawn of the twentieth century witnessed changes in almost every aspect of the day-to-day lives of women, from the domestic sphere to the public. The women's movement, with its emphasis on advocacy of equal rights, newly formed women's organisations, and the rise of a new generation of female artists, photographers and professionals, transformed the traditional patriarchal social structure across the globe. Followed closely by the advent of the First World War, these social shifts, which had been set in motion at the beginning of the century, developed further as women were propelled into the workforce and were exposed to previously male-dominated professional and political situations. Women believed that they could – and should – do whatever their male counterparts did. And when General Robert Baden-Powell started the Boy Scouts in 1907, women saw no reason why they couldn't have an equivalent organisation.

Robert Baden-Powell was the British Colonel charged with defending the town of Mafeking in South Africa during the second Boer War. The siege lasted 217 days;

Girls wearing an early version of the Guide uniform in 1910. (Copyright Girlguiding UK)

Robert Baden-Powell.
(Copyright
Girlguiding UK)

during this time, the boys of the Mafeking Cadet Corps, who are sometimes seen as a forerunner of the Scouts, were used to support the troops, carry messages, and help in the hospital. This freed up men for military duties, and kept the boys occupied. The Cadets consisted of volunteer white boys below fighting age. Their leader was thirteen-year-old Warner Goodyear, who became their Sergeant-Major. They were given khaki uniforms and wide-brimmed hats, which they wore with one side turned up; the locals often commented on their smartness. Baden-Powell had been inspired by these boys and surprised by their abilities; when he went on to found the Scouts, he was greatly influenced by them.

In 1907, Baden-Powell was inspecting seven thousand members of the Boys' Brigade in Glasgow. Sir William Smith, the founder of the Boys' Brigade, asked Baden-Powell if he had ever considered rewriting his training manual for soldiers, *Aids to Scouting for N.C.O.s and Men*, to make it relevant to young boys. (This he did: *Scouting for Boys* was published in 1908.) As a result of this conversation, Baden-Powell decided to run an experimental camp for twenty boys at Brownsea Island, Dorset, to test out his theories on providing activities for boys. Following this successful week-long camp, and the publication of *Scouting for Boys*, which became a best-seller, the Boy Scout movement swiftly established itself throughout the British Empire. The first Scout rally, held in 1909 at the Crystal Palace in London, attracted ten thousand boys – and, unexpectedly, several hundred girls. The girls were dressed in cobbled-together versions of the Scout uniform, which they had paired with skirts; many of the girls were members of girl-only Scouting groups. They asked Baden-Powell to design a programme and a uniform for them.

Doris Jourd, née Best, claimed to be the first ever Girl Guide (although officially Agnes Baden-Powell is considered to have held that title). Her mother helped the local Scoutmaster

in Gillingham, Kent, and as a result Doris attended weekly meetings and took part in Scouting activities. She asked her mother 'Why can't there be girl Scouts?' and suggested that she form a troop. Her mother had to consider the question of decorum – at the time it was considered unseemly for young ladies to engage in 'boyish' pursuits – but she finally acceded. The following morning,

The First Guides at Crystal Palace. (Copyright Girlguiding UK)

Doris bought a Boy Scout hat, a haversack and a belt. A brown blouse, a navy skirt and a broomstick made into a walking staff completed her uniform. With a copy of *Scouting for Boys* under her arm, Doris set off to recruit members for the troop. Within two weeks, over seventy girls had joined. Alice Best became the first Guide Captain and was presented with her warrant by Lord Baden-Powell at a Scout Rally in Gillingham in 1909. He said that he considered it a 'great pleasure' to be presenting the 'first warrant to a lady'. Baden-Powell had a great admiration for

women. This was probably based on the strength and fortitude of his mother, Henrietta, who raised him following his father's death, when Robert was three.

Henrietta was a remarkable woman, who excelled in music, art, languages, literature, science and mathematics. Her interests led her to establish a scheme of high school education for girls. Baden-Powell was obviously greatly affected by her influence, and in *Scouting for Boys* he noted:

> There have been women Scouts of the nation too, such as Grace Darling, who risked her life to save a shipwrecked crew; Florence Nightingale, who nursed sick soldiers in the Crimean War; Miss Kingsley, the African explorer; Lady Lugard in Africa and Alaska; and many devoted lady missionaries and nurses in all parts of our Empire. These have shown that women and girls as well as men and boys may well learn Scouting when they are young and so be able to do useful work in the world as they grow older.

This paragraph undoubtedly inspired girls to attend the rally and start their own Scout groups. Baden-Powell himself admitted how well they were suited to his Scouting programme and lamented that he hadn't found time to devise a programme for them:

> Also I have had greetings from many patrols of Girl Scouts, for which I am very grateful. They made me feel very guilty at not yet having found time to devise a scheme of Scouting better adapted for them; but I hope to get an early opportunity of starting upon it. In the meantime they seem to get a good deal of fun and instruction out of *Scouting for Boys*, and some of them are really capable Scouts.
>
> *The Scout magazine,* 16 January 1909

Girls wearing the Guide uniform in 1910. (Copyright Girlguiding UK)

After the girls' surprise attendance at the Crystal Palace rally, Baden-Powell and his sister Agnes set about adapting *Scouting for Boys* for girls: together, they wrote *How Girls Can Help to Build up the Empire* (1912). Large sections of the book remained unaltered, and it included sections on stalking, tracking, signaling and camping. Several chapters on childcare, nursing and housewifery were inserted, and stories of heroic women and girls were sometimes substituted for those centred on men and boys. The book also contained details of the enrolment ceremony, and of the second- and first-class tests which were to be the cornerstone of the Guiding programme for many years.

Agnes Baden-Powell in 1918. (Copyright Girlguiding UK)

During 1910, Robert Baden-Powell gave the new Girl Scouts the name of Girl Guides, after a famous corps of Guides that he had worked with in India who were 'distinguished for their general handiness and resourcefulness under difficulties, and their keenness and courage'. He had learnt that even when these men were 'off-duty', they still trained their minds and bodies. Therefore, he thought that 'Girl Guides' would be an excellent choice of name for these pioneering young women. Quite often, the girls were known as 'Baden-Powell Girl Guides', but they were officially called 'the Girl Guide Association'. The association grew very quickly, and Agnes Baden-Powell was made president of the new organisation, with an office in the Scout headquarters in London. Agnes became the first president of the Girl Guides when it was formed in 1910. In 1914, she started Rosebuds – later renamed Brownies – for younger girls. She stepped down as president of the Girl Guides in 1920 in favour of Robert's new wife, Olave Baden-Powell, who was named Chief Guide (for England) in 1918 and World Chief Guide in 1930.

The Boy Scouts were required to make a promise, or oath, to live up to the ideals of the movement, and subscribed to a Scout Law. It was no different for the girls. The wording of the Guide Promise and Law have varied slightly over time and from country to country, but they all feature the same principles – duty to God, to others and to self – and were inspired by the Promise and Law which were first put forward by Baden-Powell. He once wrote:

> The girls should be a feeder for the voluntary, patriotic nursing service . . . the ladies who manage this movement locally could combine it with an educative value in simultaneously appointing lady captains to raise and train companies of girls on similar principles to those given in Scouting for Boys, with details more suited to the sex.

Robert and Olave on the Arcadia *where they met and got engaged in 1912. (Copyright Girlguiding UK)*

Girls were excited by this new movement and desperately wanted to be part of it. But many of their elders felt that it was unbecoming of a young lady to roll around and play like a boy, and there was discussion of the issue within the Scout Movement. People didn't like the idea of young ladies taking part in 'boyish' activities, which were contrary to the social norms of the day. As the *Scout Headquarters Gazette* put it in 1909:

> If a girl is not allowed to run, or even hurry, to swim, ride a bike, or raise her arms above her head, how can she become a Scout?

However, Baden-Powell believed that 'girls should be partners and comrades, rather than dolls'. As the movement grew in strength, and the shadow of war loomed larger, the girls' real value became apparent.

Robert and Olave shortly after they met in 1912. (Copyright Girlguiding UK)

Chief Guide Olave Baden-Powell. (Copyright Girlguiding UK)

The girls were to be trained in the same practical and moral ways as the boys. A Tenderfoot (first level) had to know her motto – 'Be prepared' – and her Promise and Law. When she had shown that she knew these, she would be enrolled as a Guide and could move on to her second-class Guide badge, which consisted of knowledge of the Rules of the Corps, laying and lighting a fire, making a bed, cutting out and sewing a Union Jack, and being able to tie six knots. Once she had completed this, she could move on to her first-class badge. This included having one shilling in the savings bank, being able to cook a simple dish, knowing First Aid bandaging, and knowing the history of a place and acting as a guide to the place. While girls worked on their first- and second-class badges, they could also elect to do proficiency badges, which included a mix of physical activities, along with what could be seen as more traditional female pursuits. The proficiency badges included those for Ambulance, Artist, Basket Worker, Child Nurse, Cobbler, Cook, Cyclist, Dancer, Domestic Service, Entertainer, Embroiderer, Friend to Animals, Gardener, Gymnast, Handywoman, Housekeeper, Horsewoman, Interpreter, Knitter, Laundress, Milliner, Musician, Needlewoman, Naturalist, Scribe, Sick Nurse and Signaller.

By the outbreak of the First World War, Guiding and Scouting had already travelled far afield: the Girl Guides and Girl Scouts were known in most countries within the British Empire (including Ireland), in the Scandinavian countries and also in Holland, France, Switzerland, Poland and Hungary. Guiding reached the USA in 1912, when it was begun in earnest there by Juliette Low. In all these

The Chief Guide at the first World Camp at Foxlease in 1924. (Copyright Girlguiding UK)

countries, girls and women took from *Scouting for Boys* the foundations of a Promise and Law, the Patrol System and the principles behind the open-air life, and then adjusted them to their needs.

By the end of the war, it had become clear that Guiding would need to be brought under the control of some kind of international organisation. The first step on this path had been the creation of an Imperial Council in 1919, which was formed to gather information about the Guide movements that had started within the British Empire. The council would also encourage and develop the Guide movement and form a link between Guides in Britain and elsewhere, and ultimately to join them together in a sisterhood sharing the same ideas, aims and ideals. However, as work on this project began, it became evident that Guiding had moved far wider than the Commonwealth. An International Council was founded in 1919 by Olave Baden-Powell as a means of keeping in touch with members of the movement throughout the world. It was decided there that the members of this council should come together at a conference. The first International Conference of Guides was held at St Hugh's College, Oxford, in 1920. There were over one hundred council members and commissioners present. The south of Ireland was represented by the Dublin commissioners, Mrs Dixon and Miss Walker, and the county commissioner for Wicklow, Miss Scott. The north of Ireland was represented by the Duchess of Abercorn, the provincial commissioner of Ulster. There were reports by letter from those who could not attend: these included representatives from Algiers, Armenia, Argentina, Brazil, Turkey, Czecho-slovakia, Japan, Palestine and Peru. At the Fifth International Conference in Hungary in 1928, delegates formed the World Association of Girl Guides and Girl Scouts (WAGGGS), which replaced the International Council.

The first conference discussed what were to become the cornerstones of the Guide movement. There were discussions on the origin, ideals and organisation of the movement, the training of Guiders, the powers and duties of commissioners, the role of 'play' in education, ceremonies (the USA introduced 'Taps', a now-traditional song sung at the end of Guide meetings, at this conference), Brownie Branch and Senior Guides (it was at this point that the name 'Rangers' was decided on). Lady Baden-Powell said that the role of the International Council was not that of organisation but to 'tell how and in what way the system of training has been successful here, and hope that they [the

Overleaf: *Lord and Lady Baden-Powell with their family in 1933. (Copyright Girlguiding UK)*

various national organisations] may feel inclined to adopt it too'. The Honorary Secretary of the Council, Mrs Essex Reade said: 'personally, I look upon this international side of Guiding as a sort of Junior League of Nations, and think it has a tremendous future before it and a great power for good'. She went on to endorse the 'Post Box', a pen-pal program which encouraged girls from different countries all over the world to correspond with their counterparts in other organisations. It was felt that the conference was so successful that one should be held every two years from then on. Conferences were held every two years (except during the Second World War) until 1954, when it was decided to hold them every three years; there have been thirty-three World Conferences to date.

The movement flourished with the Baden-Powells at its helm and now, a hundred years later, the World Association of Girl Guides and Girl Scouts is an umbrella organisation with 10 million members in 145 countries. Like the Scout movement before it, the Guides captured the imaginations of children and adults alike. Since 1909, approximately 250 million women have worked through the Girl Guide programme worldwide. The seed planted in a dedicated few at the Crystal Palace in 1909 grew to become the worldwide phenomenon that we know today.

CHAPTER 2

The Start of a Great Adventure

Irish women in the early twentieth century had very few rights and were often treated as second-class citizens. Most women only attended to primary school, with a very small percentage attending second level and even fewer attending third level. Careers outside the home for women were few and far between, as women were generally expected to stay at home and rear children. Many women married young and were encouraged to have large families. At the same time as Baden-Powell was starting his new movements for boys and girls, the suffragette movement was gaining momentum in England and Ireland. The suffragists – who were often militant in their expressions of protest – presented a sometimes stark contrast to the feminine ideal of the era, which portrayed women as delicate, demure and silent, confined to a domestic world that cocooned them from the harsh realities of the world. Women worldwide were challenging traditional views. Moreover, the women of Ireland also had to deal with a backdrop of Ireland's rapidly changing political life, which was directly tied to notions of national identity.

A Greystones Brownie in 1921.

The idea of youth movements and organisations was very much in its infancy in the early 1900s, and there were very few organisations which young women could join. The Scout movement was founded in 1907 by Robert Baden-Powell and in the following year the first troop had been started in Ireland. There were some organisations which catered for girls, but they tended to be associated with a particular religious denomination. For instance, the Girls' Brigade, a Christian youth organisation for girls, had been active in Ireland since 1893. It was founded on the twin pillars of Bible class and physical training. The aim of the Brigade was 'the extension of Christ's Kingdom among Girls'. The Girls' Friendly Society, another religious organisation, had been present in Ireland since 1877. In 1909, the St John's Ambulance Brigade of Ireland allowed women to join, but this organisation appealed mostly to those who were interested in medicine or nursing.

When the Guides started in Ireland, it lit a fire amongst Irish girls and women, as it, by contrast with the organisations mentioned above, covered a multitude of activities and skills. Girls saw an opportunity to act like boys, to run and play and act in a manner none of the other organisations would allow. It was also non-denominational, which meant that girls from all backgrounds could join. Guiding and Scouting were new and innovative, and catered for girls of all interests, abilities and backgrounds.

> My friends and I started as Girl Scouts about 1913. We got our mother to make us khaki shirts and we bought Scouts' hats for 2s 6d each. At that time we considered ourselves to be very much part of the British Empire and we used to tie the Union Jack to our bicycles. However, as soon as the Girl Guides heard about us they gathered us

into their movement. This was the beginning of a forty-year association with the Guide movement. It was a terrific character-building organisation.

Sheila Findlater

—◦◦◦—

News of this exciting new movement reached Ireland in 1911, and took hold there quickly. It operated under the umbrella of the UK association and 'headquarters' was in London. The first Guide company set up in Ireland was in Harold's Cross in Dublin in September 1911 by a Miss Bayham. However, Miss Bayham never enrolled as a Guide (there is no indication as to the reason why), and the company's first Guide Mistress was Miss Ethel Tisdall, who remained with the company until 1919. The company was known as the 1st South Dublin Company, and they met weekly in the Harold's Cross Parochial Hall on Leinster Road West. The 1st South Dublin was quickly followed by St Peter's (1st City Company) in 1912; Sandford and Cork in 1913; Rathgar and Limerick (St Michael's) in 1914; and Zion (based in Rathgar and still in existence), Borris (Carlow), Waterford and Abbey Street (Dublin) in 1915. By the end of 1915, there were also four units in Belfast, two in Portadown, and one each in Ballycastle, Clifden, Limerick, Portarlington, Newbridge, Waterford and Sligo.

In 1912, Mrs Margaret Dixon and her husband (a professor of anatomy at Trinity College) became interested in Guiding and Scouting and both became longstanding members of the respective movements in Ireland. Mrs Dixon was asked to form a committee to foster Guiding in Ireland; the first meetings of this committee were held in her house in Grosvenor Road in Rathgar, Dublin. She

1st Company Group – St Peter's - St Matthias' Parish 1919.

began the first county branch of the Guides in Dublin and was, at first, both secretary and county commissioner (from 1914). In 1917, the first list of commissioners was published by Headquarters in London; it showed commissioners for Dublin, Louth, Kildare, Antrim, Belfast and Down, and the city of Derry. Mrs Dixon believed it was important that companies should follow the non-sectarian, non-denominational model which had been laid down by Baden-Powell. She wrote:

> the good work done among the girls by means of this movement was very noticeable. It helped them to become useful members of the home, and more conscientious and responsible in any occupation they took up. They were also encouraged to attend the technical schools, where they learned cooking, dressmaking and so forth.

—∿∿—

Guiding continued to flourish, and another major step was taken with the establishment of the Rosebuds (later the Brownies). Lord Baden-Powell founded the Rosebuds when it became clear to him that the younger sisters of Guides and Scouts would benefit from being involved with the organisation. They are first mentioned at an investiture (enrolment of members) in Newbridge, County Kildare, in 1914. The *Girl Guides Gazette* (the official publication of the Girl Guides from 1913) suggested that Rosebuds wear a dark blue skirt, knitted jersey, cap or tam, and the Rosebud brooch. At first, Rosebuds didn't have a programme to follow like the Brownies of today. However, they, along with the Guides, contributed to their local community by doing things such as collecting clothing and household items for the war effort. A Rosebud was expected to know how the Union Jack was folded and how to fly it; how to tie a reef knot, sheetbend, clove hitch, bowline, sheepshank and fisherman's knot; and how to do bending exercises.

The outbreak of the First World War provided Guides and Scouts with an ideal theatre to showcase their skills and use them in a practical way. In Ireland, they collected sphagnum moss and made it into dressings. They also knitted for soldiers and acted as hospital orderlies and helped in canteens. A new badge, the War Service Badge, was created to encourage girls to help in the war effort. In order to gain this badge, the Guide had to give at least twenty-one days' service to a hospital or similar institution, or knit at least fifteen articles, which had to include socks, mittens, shirts, pyjamas, a belt and a bed jacket. Various fund-raising and relief efforts were organised throughout the country: in Portarlington, there was a sale of work; numerous Dublin Companies were involved in sewing for Belgian refugees; and Guides in Bray knitted blankets for the troops.

1st Dublin Brownies in 1919.

In the early days we learnt skills like bed making – no duvets in those days – and First Aid. We used to help out in Linden Convalescent home in Stillorgan, where wounded soldiers were recovering. We were used as patients for First Aid and home nursing classes given by doctors when war was declared.

Sheila Findlater

By 1915, the Guides had become very visible to the people of Ireland, and this was heralded by a number of large-scale public events. There were three hundred Guides divided into companies in various parts of Dublin, and on 23 April over two hundred of these Guides came together and gave a display in the Metropolitan Hall in Abbey Street. Lady Powerscourt and Lady Holmpatrick (vice-presidents of the Dublin Branch) attended. Lady Powerscourt read a telegram from Lord Baden-Powell congratulating the Dublin Guides on their numbers and efficiency. In June, the County Dublin Girl Guides took part in the St John's Ambulance review in Iveagh Gardens. In a feature on the review published on 26 June, the *Irish Times* noted:

Harold's Cross Brownies in 1925.

> [these] are the Ambulance and Red Cross recruits of the future . . . the ideals of the movement are to create in young girls a public spirit [and] usefulness and accustom them to discipline . . . and the rules provide that they are not allowed to parade the streets with boys nor loaf about – on the contrary they are encouraged in every way to retain their womanliness, so that they may be good mothers and good Guides to the next generation.

Mrs Dixon of the Dublin Guides published an article in the *Irish Times* setting out the origins and ethos of Guiding in Dublin. She discussed how to set up a new company and stressed the importance of good officers:

> The first essential [when setting up a Guide company] is the senior officer. There is no doubt there would be Guides in many more districts

if it were not so difficult to find a sufficient number of suitable officers. It needs a thoroughly competent, sympathetic and unselfish girl to make a good officer. But this difficulty is not insurmountable, and the successful officer always finds herself more than repaid for any sacrifices she has made on behalf of her Guides.

Irish Times, 3 July 1915

In August of that year, the Baden-Powells paid their first visit to Ireland and attended a rally in Merrion Square, where they inspected both Guides and Scouts. There were about two hundred Guides present. This visit raised the profile of Guiding in Ireland, and numbers continued to increase, particularly outside Dublin. Audrey Murphy (née O'Callaghan) remembers joining a 'well-established Company' in Tralee in 1915. The unit, which was run by Captain Miss Alice Rohan, met in rooms on Denny Street in Tralee, once a week. She recalls:

I remember Swimming, Sailing, Running and Jumping, 1st Aid [these were some of the badges Audrey would have worked towards] etc. As it was during the war, we did work for the Red Cross. I remember collecting eggs, silver paper and ends of wax candles for soap or polish, also cowslips for cowslip wine. Older Guides knitted socks for the Red Cross. In summer we collected seashells, which we made into things in the winter months. We also collected mushrooms, which we made into ketchup and sold for company funds. I remember learning bandaging using our ties. We did Morse signalling, which was very popular. We went on hikes, especially to a place called Sally's Rock. We did tracking, outdoor fires, tent pitching, collecting wild flowers, pressed leaves, etc. I remember bird-watching and finding our way back from mountain walks by a map. We also went on expeditions on our bicycles. It was all great fun and I was sorry to have to leave in 1917 when I went away to school.

—◊◊◊—

The 1916 Rising provided another platform for the women of Ireland to step onto a national stage and prove that they were equal to men when it came to both wartime service and politics. Women were mentioned as equals in Padraig Pearse's Proclamation and fought in the GPO alongside James Connolly and Pearse. In short, they were starting to play a full and important part in politics; this inspired the young women of Ireland, including those in the new Girl Guide movement.

The Guides attempted, successfully, to remain neutral during hostilities. They were at their core a youth movement and remained apolitical. During these troubled times, the Guides carried on with their usual training and other activities. They held rallies and competitions and gave entertainments to raise funds for themselves and, often, for war-relief projects.

The Dublin Girl Guides' Association numbered twenty companies by 1917, with several new companies in the pipeline. According to the annual report for that year, 'the number would be even greater if there were an adequate supply of

Officers. We would appeal to those interested in the Girl Guides to help us by making this need widely known'.

Examinations for proficiency badges continued to be held. Many of the badges earned were similar to those earned by today's Guides and Brownies, but some, such as Cobbler, Milliner, Sick Nurse, Clerk, Milkmaid and War Service, were specific to the early twentieth century. Gaining a badge was no easy feat. A Board of Examiners was appointed in each district to 'ensure standardisation of tests in that District'. 'Candidates for Proficiency Tests must be either First or Second Class Guides' and 'a high standard of efficiency should be aimed at, but the actual test should be based on the amount of individual effort expended on the work by the Guide'. (*Hints on Girl Guide Badges*, 14th ed., 1931) The child-centred approach of the last line shows how advanced the Guide movement was from the beginning.

In 1918, the Chief Guide, Lady Baden-Powell, decided that in order to facilitate the smooth running of the association, she should have a deputy in each country in the United Kingdom. She chose Lady Powerscourt for this position in Ireland. Lady Powerscourt duly accepted, and began the work of appointing commissioners. Each province had a commissioner, with the Duchess of Abercorn representing Ulster, Mrs Hignett, Leinster, and Lady de Freyne, Connacht. Munster does not seem to have had a commissioner until the Countess of Kenmare took up the position in 1929. However, due to the political situation in Ireland, Ulster was removed permanently from

Opposite:
A Guide in 1916.

Lady Powerscourt
leaving Leinster
House in 1919.

Guides at Leinster House in 1919.

Lady Powerscourt's sphere of influence in 1920 following the Government of Ireland Act, which created a separate state of Northern Ireland, consisting of the six north-eastern counties of Ulster, and proposed separate parliaments for Northern Ireland and Southern Ireland. However, the Duchess of Abercorn retained her position, and Guiding on both sides of the new border remained linked.

The First World War did not stop Guide meetings from being held, and in 1918 there was a rally held for Scouts and Guides. At this rally, the Ross Cup was presented to Lady Ross. The cup was then to be presented in her name to an individual Guide between the ages of fourteen and nineteen 'for excellence in needlework, child hygiene and meatless cookery'. Various competitions were held every year for individuals and units; these included the Leinster Challenge Shield, the Dublin Banner and the Wicklow Shield. The friendly rivalry between areas stimulated plenty of good fun.

Work continued on the war effort. According to the third annual report of the Girl Guides (Dublin Branch):

> War Work done by the Guides has been on the same lines as described in our last report, namely helping the Red Cross and St John Ambulance Societies by acting as orderlies, replacing V.A.D. workers on holidays, distributing leaflets and collecting waste paper. The Guides services have been increasingly asked for, and it is gratifying to receive the good reports of the work done by them.

Lady Powerscourt presenting the Ross Cup.

Nineteen eighteen also saw the first Irish group to camp under canvas. It was frowned upon for girls to camp, as it was seen to be unladylike, but Miss Figgis of Greystones Company thought differently. She was told that if she obtained written permission from the parents of each girl, then they could camp. Writing in 1957, Miss Figgis remembered:

> For our cooking at both our first two camps, we had two fires, one with a tripod of staves rigged over it, from which hung a pot or kettle, according to the meal being prepared; we fried on the other. Lats [latrines]? We dug a hole in the middle of a group of trees, twined string round the trunks and tucked in bracken fronds to make a screen; these had to be added to nearly every day! When no more holes could be dug, we did the same around another set of trees. Washing? This was long before 'summer time' was invented. It was dark at bedtime, so we all went together to a little stream in the woods where, hidden by the bushes, we each selected a stone for our clothes and washed, standing in the ice-cold water. It was much nicer than any wash shelter!
>
> *Trefoil News*, June 1957

Former chief commissioner Eileen Beatty has fond memories of camping:

> Camping at that time was not considered to be very safe so for several years the Dublin Committee took an empty house at Kilternan for the summer months and we thoroughly enjoyed what we would now call

indoor camping, sleeping in the house but eating outside when possible. My recollection is that we were no quieter at night than are some of the Guides today, and I well remember the 'shushing' when Captain was heard approaching to give us a piece of her mind! I also seem to remember treating our Guiders with great respect and consideration, the polishing of their badges and shoes etc, and it didn't do us any harm either! Camps were sometimes held in the yard at Powerscourt but one of our best milestones was when we were first allowed to camp under canvas. This is perhaps the great highlight for a Guide – her first camp. And some of the happiest days of my life have been spent in camp, especially Guiders' training camps, with good friends, fun, and the endless joy of living out of doors.

Trefoil News, 1957

Once the initial ban was lifted at the end of the decade, camping became an integral part of Guiding for girls and leaders alike. Most units tried to camp at least once a year, and many used camping as an opportunity to team up with other units for fun and adventures. The adventures were getting more and more exciting, and it became clear to leaders that Guides were becoming reluctant to leave their company once they reached the age of sixteen, so many companies started to form Senior Patrols for the older girls. In June 1917, Baden-Powell had asked Rose Kerr to take on responsibility for them, outlining to her a plan for them. This began to catch on, and from 1918 'The Scheme for Senior Girls' was serialised in the *Girl Guides Gazette*. Many names were suggested for these older girls but it was the Chief Guide who came up with the name 'Rangers', which stuck and is indeed still used today. She said:

Guides on washing-up duty at camp in the 1920s.

> Here is the suggested new name: 'Ranger'. If you look it up in the dictionary, you will find it means quite a number of things. 'To range' is 'to set in proper order'; 'to roam' . . . might well mean you are going to tread ground as a Senior Guide that as a Guide you have not yet passed. 'Distance of vision, and extent of discourse or roaming power' again shows that as a senior member of the community you are expected to look farther afield for good, and the work that you can do for the community. 'To range' means to travel, or to rove over wide distances, whether in your mind or your body. A Ranger is 'one who guards a large tract of land or forest', thus it comes to mean one who has a wide outlook, and a sense of responsible protective duties, appropriate to a Senior Guide. Another definition is 'to sail along in a parallel direction', and so we can feel that the Ranger Guides are complementary to the Rover Scouts. And so we hope that this new title will have the approval of all.
>
> *The Girl Guide Gazette*, June 1920

The first Ranger unit in Ireland was called 13th Dublin (St Stephen's); the leader was Miss F. M. Drew. Originally there were three branches for older girls – Rangers, Cadets (who trained for service in the Girl Guide movement) and Sea Guides – but they all joined under the name 'Ranger' in 1927.

With the end of the First World War, the War Service badge was discontinued. Nonetheless, it was reported in the 1918 annual report that:

> Brownies have flourished exceedingly, and at present nearly every Guide Company runs a Brownie pack. They have now their own handbook, Brownies and Bluebirds, and have grown to be very important little people.

The period between the two world wars was one of huge expansion for the Girl Guides in Ireland. The movement had moved into all twenty-six counties in the South by the end of the 1920s. In the Dublin Branch (which was still the predominant area) alone, there were twenty-seven companies: there were 23 Rangers, 620 Guides, 204 Brownies and 64 Guiders. Training for leaders was an important part of the curriculum: it was deemed essential to keep them abreast of changes in the association. The first

training week for Guiders was held over Easter in the Clergy Daughters School in Dublin and Miss Bewley, the head of Rangers, travelled from headquarters in London to train the Irish leaders.

Gatherings would continue to be disrupted in Ireland following the turmoil associated with the War of Independence and the civil war. In the 1921–1922 annual report of the Dublin Branch, it was reported that 'owing to disturbed conditions the Summer Rally was not held and for the same reason the Guiders' Training week and the Summer Camp at Powerscourt were abandoned'. It was

A Summer Rally in Lord Iveagh's grounds.

difficult for the Guides to meet in public, especially in uniform, as there was a deep distrust of uniformed organisations at that time. Company meetings were held irregularly, and quietly. Guiding remained strong in Dublin but struggled in other counties. By 1923, it was still 'considered inadvisable to hold the Summer Rally', presumably due to the ongoing tensions following the civil war. Although these tensions restricted Guides' public displays, companies still managed to meet. One Guide from Leeson Park, Patricia Boate, said she was so keen on Guides 'that I used to spend the night before Guides polishing my stars, my badge and my belt. I polished it so much, all the decoration was gone from it. One day I even walked to Guides so I wouldn't crease my uniform before inspection'. During this period, there are records of Good Turns, rallies, inter-company competitions and trainings for Guiders and Patrol leaders. The civil war didn't stop

Guides travelling abroad and, in July 1923 (two months after the end of the civil war), 260 Guides went to a camp in Wales for a week, staying at Morfa Hut Camp.

By 1924, the Dublin Branch had grown to 1,330 members – a figure that rose steadily every year. The annual summer rally was reinstated in 1924, after not having been held in 1922 and 1923. A training camp was held in Santry; this marked the beginning of intensive yearly training of all Guiders. Lord Powerscourt made his estate available for camps throughout the summer.

Camp Conway in Wales, 1923.

The first World Camp was held in Foxlease in England in 1924, in conjunction with the third world conference. Delegates from all the Guiding countries attended, and around one thousand campers slept under canvas. The cost for food per person for the week was 8s 6d. The leftover food was either returned to the shop, sold to the housekeeper at Foxlease, or given to the cottages on the estate; the bread was taken away by the Southampton workhouse bread cart and given to the poor. Mrs Cerise Parker (née Orpen) wrote to her mother from camp, saying:

> Tuesday – there are so many things to say I don't know where to begin but I have arrived safely . . . In the next tent there are two Polish Guides jabbering away, they are very friendly and speak jolly well in broken English . . . I hear that by tomorrow there will be 1097 Guides . . . Tomorrow evening there is to be a huge Campfire and Sir Robert Baden-Powell is to come down. At the International Evenings each country has to perform an evening. Ireland is joining up with Ulster.

*A Commissioner
putting up a tent.*

Also in 1924, Lady Powerscourt invited all the Dublin Guides and Guiders to a picnic on the estate. The same year, the first Jewish company was opened in Dublin; it was run by Jewish officers specifically for Jewish girls. Guiding in the south of the country had started to flourish as well; in Cork, Mrs Leigh-White held Captains' Meetings at Rochelle School. This seems to be the beginning of Cork's central organisation as a county; there had previously been references to individuals and companies in Cork but nothing about a county committee. Mrs Leigh-White is referred to as the county commissioner until 1930, when she became the deputy chief commissioner. From the beginning, Cork put a great emphasis on camping: copies of early minutes are full of references to campsites, funds, equipment, suitable Guiders and numbers of Guides for each camp (for which only enrolled Guides were eligible). Camp requirements were discussed, and a list of songs and rounds for camp was made out, with copies sent to every company involved. General trainings, both whole- and half-day, were also organised. There is evidence that Dublin and Cork were in communication and were attending each other's trainings. The invitations were sent by telegram.

Lone Guides began in Ireland around this time. Lone Guides, or 'Lones', were Girl Guides who did not attend group meetings for a variety of reasons – for example geographical isolation, lack of like-minded people in their area or work commitments. They were organised into groups that kept in touch. A Lone group consisted of not less than four members, living in the same district and able to meet occasionally. Members carried out their organisation's normal programme on their own, as much as they were able. The first official Lone Guides started in 1912 in the UK, and there were Irish members in that group. The unit continued until 1925, when it had an Irish leader, but had begun to dissipate and was to be disbanded. However, it was agreed to keep it open in order to allow the Irish members to meet. In 1927, the 2nd South Irish Lones was formed, and in the same year the first Lone Secretary for Southern Ireland was appointed. Two years later, County Meath started a Lone Company.

In 1932, the first provincial Lone Company was started, with members coming from Cork and Kerry. The logbook of the 1st Munster Lones contains the captain's letters to her girls, in which she passes on new assignments, comments on those that were sent to her, and gives information about outings and camps. It was an essential guide for the Lones, who were cut off from more conventional units.

In 1925, Mrs Margaret Dixon, one of the founding members of Guiding in Ireland, resigned her position as commissioner of County Dublin. The 'Dixon Fund' was created in order to send one Guider from County Dublin to Foxlease for training every year; this was the first of many funds that were set up over the years in order to further international and training opportunities.

In November 1925, the Chief Guide, Lady Baden-Powell, visited Ireland. There was not enough time for her to meet all the Guides and Guiders but rooms were taken in the Mansion House and an informal reception was held (for officers only). In the evening, a rally was held in the Round Room of the Mansion House.

Guides gathered in the Metropolitan Hall in 1925.

Lady Baden-Powell was presented with a dress length of Irish poplin as a memento of her visit.

The fourth world conference was held in the USA in 1926; it was here that the idea of Thinking Day was put forward. This would be a day when all Guides around the world thought of one another and commemorated the day in some special way. It was considered to be an excellent idea; the date chosen was 22

February – the joint birthday of Lord and Lady Baden-Powell. The day would also be used to raise funds to develop Guiding around the world. The first Thinking Day was held in 1927.

In August 1927, an International Camp was held in Geneva. The Guides of the South of Ireland were invited to send five Guides and one Guider. Four Guides went from Dublin and one from Wicklow, with Miss Figgis (the County Camp Advisor for Wicklow and Captain of Greystones Company) in charge.

The organisation's popularity continued to increase, and fourteen camps were held during the summer of 1928. By far the biggest event in the Guiding and Scouting Calendar that year was the visit of the Chief Scout and Chief Guide; rallies were organised in Cork and Dublin to celebrate the visit. The Dublin rally was held in Lansdowne Road on 15 August. The programme included a Grand Salute, a march past the grandstand, singing and dancing by Brownies, and physical exercises and Irish dances by the Guides. This was followed by a speech from the Chief Guide. All music was provided by the Garda Síochána (Depot) Band. Over two thousand Brownies, Guides, Rangers and Guiders were present to salute the Chiefs. The winner of the Leinster Shield, County Dublin Banner, GFS Shield and County Wicklow Shield were presented with their prizes. Lady Baden-Powell, in her address to the Guides present, said

Lord and Lady Baden-Powell at a Rally in Lansdowne Road in 1928.

that she was very happy indeed to have the chance of visiting the Guides in Dublin again. Since her last visit, they had grown in size and excellence, and she was proud to say that she had never seen a better rally in any part of the world (*Evening Herald*, 16 August 1928). The evening ended with 'God Save the King' and the Free State anthem, and a salute to Lord and Lady Baden-Powell. Even with all this excitement and activity, there were still trips overseas, and in July the Dublin Branch was invited to combine with Ulster in staffing the Irish Group at the Imperial Camp at Foxlease.

The Guide movement in Ireland tended, in the early days, to be predominantly Protestant and to be seen as associated with the British establishment. In reaction to this, a similar association was founded in 1928 to cater to the needs of Catholic girls only. This new organisation was called Clanna Bhríde; the name was changed to the Catholic Girl Guides of Ireland in 1932. They had a similar uniform to the Guides but wore brown instead of blue – and became known colloquially as the 'Brown Guides'. The Catholic movement spread into the provinces, notably to Cork, Limerick and Waterford, but as it was not a member of WAGGGS, its members could not attend international Guiding events.

In the beginning, the Catholic movement had no central governance. In 1972, the federation of the Catholic Girl Guides of Ireland was formed; initially, the federation represented the Dioceses of Cork & Ross, Down & Connor, Dublin, Ferns, and Waterford & Lismore. Later, they were joined by the Dioceses of Armagh, Clogher and Derry & Raphoe. In 1977, the federation became a national organisation: the Catholic Guides of Ireland. (CGI)

The foundation of a Catholic Guiding movement probably emerged from an anti-Protestant/anti-British sentiment that was all-pervasive in Ireland at the time.

The Irish Free State Guides had Catholic, Protestant and Jewish members (in 1932, they were a major part of the Eucharistic Congress). They had been founded as a non-denominational organisation and tried to maintain that ethos, but as the organisation had started in Britain and was closely associated with Headquarters in London, the perception was that it was an English Protestant organisation. The War of Independence and the civil war had created major divisions throughout the country, and the Guide movement was by no means the only organisation that saw a split along sectarian lines: the Boy Scouts had gone through a similar split in 1926, leading to the foundation of the Catholic Boy Scouts of Ireland.

In 1929, Lord and Lady Baden-Powell continued their tour of Guiding and Scouting countries, and in June they attended a rally at Balmoral, Belfast. According to the *Irish Times*, this rally would 'commemorate the coming-of-age of the Scout movement'. Special attractions included folk dancing, a combined Guide and Scout choir and military bands. Eleven thousand Boy Scouts and Girl Guides welcomed the Chief Guide and Chief Scout. The *Irish Times* reported that, in her speech, Lady Baden-Powell said that 'Girl Guides are like ships. They sent out messages of goodwill and of hope to every corner of the globe, and like the ships, they were rendering great service to mankind'.

The same year, a new era in Irish Guiding began when the Irish Free State Girl Guides were born. This made sense, as the Free State had been in place since 1922 and other dominions had already founded their own independent associations. The new association was no longer run from London and had its own constitution and council . It was the beginning of a new and exciting time for Guiding in Ireland.

CHAPTER 3

The Irish Free State Girl Guides

The late twenties and early thirties were a period of great upheaval in Ireland and, by extension, in Irish Guiding. Ireland had been divided into North and South as a result of Dominion status, which was introduced in 1922. The country was still part of the British Commonwealth of Nations but had control of its own internal affairs. However, Girl Guides in Ireland had made no attempt to change their own structures, and it was Lady Baden-Powell, during a visit in 1928, who suggested that the Girl Guides in Southern Ireland should seek Dominion status. Within WAGGGS, moves needed to be made to create a new organisation. She noted in a letter to Mrs Leigh-White in 1929 that she was glad that the latter was 'satisfied about this plan for the Irish Free State Guides'. This status would put them on the same footing as organisations in Canada, South Africa and Australia. The next two years would be dedicated to creating a new national organisation, which would be known as the Irish Free State Girl Guides (IFSGG).

The presentation of the Chief Commissioner's Banner in 1936.

The Irish Free State Girl Guides' Trefoil.

Flag of the Irish Girl Guides from 1971

In 1929, the Irish Girl Guides began the process of separating from the UK Guide Association, with the intention of drawing up a new constitution and forming a General Council tailored to the administration of Guiding in the Free State. Lady Sybil Powerscourt was appointed as the new organisation's first chief commissioner. The Guide flag featured the new Cross of St Patrick, with the World Guide Badge in the centre. The cross symbolises unity, peace and concord. A number of distinctly Irish items were added to the test work, such as badges for Irish Speaking and Irish Traditional Dancing. The first annual report of the new organisation records a membership of 3,493 for the twenty-six counties. This statistic was referred to by Lady Sybil Powerscourt in her foreword to the 1930 annual report:

> I feel that the publishing of the first annual report of the Irish Girl Guides is of such importance that I cannot let it pass without a few words of congratulations and appreciation. Congratulations to commissioners, Guiders and Guides on the way in which they have not only maintained but made progress with their Guide work during the past two years, in spite of the fact that during that period the organisation in this country has been passing through a stage of transition.

In 1931, Baden-Powell sent a letter to Lady Powerscourt informing her that she, Lady Powerscourt, had been elected as a member of the Council of the Girl Guides Association. This was in order to provide 'a closer link between . . . Headquarters and the Guide Associations in the Dominions'.

The next step in the formation of an independent association was to present it to the world. The IFSGG was represented at the world conference of Girl Guides and Girl Scouts in Poland in 1932 by Frances Daly (later Frances Dwyer, chief commissioner from 1980 to 1987). Ireland became a separate member of the World Association of Girl Guides and Girl Scouts (WAGGGS) at this conference. There were to have been two delegates, but due to the illness of Miss Scott, Frances Daly was sent to Poland on her own. She confessed to being nervous but said that once she 'arrived in Poland and settled down in that delightfully friendly atmosphere, everybody was so nice that I quite forgot to be afraid about anything'.

Lady Powerscourt sewing a carpet in the 1930s.

The conference was opened with a campfire, and at the opening ceremony each participant was given a wooden vessel filled with some oil and a tiny wick. Once the Chief Guide had lit the campfire, all the participants were asked in turn to pour the oil on the fire, to symbolise all the nations adding their share to the big flame of Guiding. Ms Daly commented that the other delegates were fascinated by the Irish Free State badge and thought it was a good idea to have a distinguishing badge for each country. The Irish Girl Guides continued to send a full delegation to the triennial world conferences of WAGGGS until 1993 (when the Council of Irish Guiding Associations, discussed below, was formed).

The IFSGG's first official outing was at the opening of Our Chalet in Adelboden. Our Chalet was the first of what would eventually amount to four world 'houses' for Girl Guides. The building was given to WAGGGS by Helen Storrow of the USA. The following international motto was quoted by the Guide who represented the Irish Free State at the opening:

From the blue hills of Eire come the legends of the heroes and the visions of the Saints. With the Blessing of St Patrick, the Irish Girl Guides will keep shining brightly the light of his message to the World: Unity, Peace and Concord.

———∾∾∾———

Application for the opening of Our Chalet in 1932.

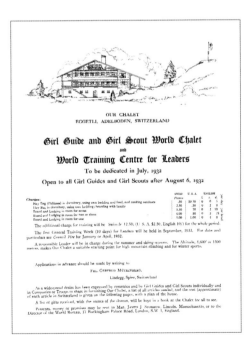

Nineteen thirty-two was a pivotal year for Irish Guiding, as the organisation developed its international profile. Not only had they been presented to the International Conference and at Our Chalet, but the IFSGG also hosted Ireland's first International Camp (a tradition which has continued to the present). The camp was held in conjunction with the 31st International Eucharistic Congress, which was held in Dublin in June 1932. This event was hugely significant in terms of asserting the identity of the Irish Free State as a leading Catholic nation. It was the largest public spectacle in twentieth-century Ireland.

Not since the War of Independence and the civil war had the international spotlight been so obviously trained on Ireland; the IFSGG saw it as an ideal opportunity to showcase their prowess at organising large-scale public events. Rangers offered to staff the camp, which was held in Powerscourt, and run activities. They were asked to cut and stack wood and to build a shed where cars could be parked. The cost of the camp was £1.05 for ten days. There were eight group camps, with about twenty-two girls and four staff for each camp. The kit list was much the same as today's kit lists – with a few notable differences. The girls in 1932 were asked to bring a palliasse, described as a 'case for filling with straw; straw will be provided'. They were also asked to bring shoe-cleaning and badge-cleaning equipment.

The Saint Columcille Group (one of the sub-groups at the camp) kept a booklet of their programme and activities; this booklet gives great insights into the goings-on during the ten-day camp. Saint Columcille was made up of Irish, English, Finnish, American and Scottish campers. The programme was packed, with the cooks getting up at 7AM and serving breakfast to the other campers at 8.45AM. At 10.15, colours (the flag ceremony) were presented, followed by prayers. At 10.30, there was an inspection, and at 11 canteen was available. Dinner was served at 1PM and rest hour was between 2 and 3PM. A group went into Dublin at 2PM and other more local expeditions left the site at 2.30PM. Tea was served at 4.15 and supper at 7.15; this was followed by a campfire. After the campfire, there were prayers, and lights-out was at 10.15PM. The whole camp attended the Congress Masses, which were held in the Phoenix Park on the Saturday and Sunday of Camp. Powerscourt was ideal for such a large scale camp – a fact that was acknowledged by participants:

Group of International Girl Guides. Powerscourt. Eucharistic Congress Dublin 1932

Relaxing at the Eucharistic Congress Camp.

It would be hard to imagine a more ideal site for a group camp than the one chosen for us at Powerscourt. In spite of our great numbers, there was a feeling of space, and each group was like a separate camp. 'St Columcille' was lucky enough to get first choice of the sites, and was situated next to HQ, on the highest point of the field, with a wonderful view across the Wicklow Mountains.

Saint Columcille Camp Logbook

Mrs Leigh White and Miss Scott at the Eucharistic Congress Camp.

The weather for the camp was fine for the whole time. As Ms Butler of the USA put it: 'Old man sunshine was most cordially invited and without coaxing graciously accepted.' Several off-site expeditions were arranged; these included trips to Dublin, Glendalough, Kilruddery and Bray (for swimming). Campfires were held every night, and Lady Powerscourt always attended. Dancing and singing lessons were given by the different nationalities present. The weather finally broke on the last day of camp, and there was an impressive thunderstorm as the girls packed their belongings. The 8 o'clock bus for the Cork girls did not arrive until 11, but this news was met with loud cheers at the prospect of a few extra hours at camp. A contingent went to Kingstown (Dun Laoghaire) to see off the boats and 'slowly the boat steamed off; we cheered and cheered again, louder and louder as the distance increased, and kept on cheering wildly till we could no longer hear the answering cries' (Saint Columcille Camp Logbook). Ireland's first International Camp had been a huge success.

Also in 1932 (a very busy year), the 21st anniversary of Guiding was celebrated with 'Guide Week' from 21 to 28 June. There were special church parades and various forms of public and private Good Turns. The celebrations culminated in a Thanksgiving Service held in St Patrick's Cathedral in Dublin.

The following year, possibly in an attempt to assert its newly found independence, the IFSGG sent a team of Irish dancers to the World Scout and Guide Folk Dancing Festival. There was widespread praise for these dancers, including a mention in the *Sunday Independent*:

The Irish team at the Folk Dance Festival in London in 1933.

> I had an opportunity of seeing a charming and accomplished performance by the full Irish team; and I have no hesitation in saying it was one of the finest exhibitions of Irish National Dancing ever seen in London, and the loud applause at the close of the performance showed how highly it was appreciated. . . . It is pleasing to record that the national garb of the twelve *cailíní* from Ireland with its saffron and blue was among the most beautiful and graceful of the feminine costumes.
>
> *Sunday Independent,* 16 July 1933

Lord Baden-Powell also congratulated the organisation of the event, and the dancers themselves:

> I cannot resist writing to offer to yourself and to your team of dancers my very cordial congratulations on your delightful performance at the World Scout and Guide Folk Dancing Festival.
>
> It was a most unique and really wonderful exhibition and charmed all of us who saw it.
>
> With sincere congratulations,
>
> Yours sincerely,
>
> Baden-Powell of Gilwell

Up to 1935, Irish Guiding had no national headquarters. In October of that year, the Executive Committee decided to look for suitable premises; at their meeting in November, it was announced that Lady Powerscourt had successfully negotiated the lease of the top floor of 5 Dawson Street. The Irish Free State Guides spent a year at 5 Dawson Street, their first headquarters. The office was sparse to begin with but thanks to many kind benefactors it soon began to feel like home, and in November:

> our only piece of furniture, a very small cupboard, was triumphantly removed [to Dawson Street]. Our spirits were then raised by the gift of a cheerful roll of carpeting from the deputy chief commissioner. . . . The chief commissioner presented curtains and an invaluable table to which Mrs Lombard Murphy

added a cloth, Lady Walsh a blotter and Miss de Selby an inkstand. To her we also owe gratitude for a charming little picture, and to Lady Murphy for a clock, to Miss Kenny for bookshelves, to Miss Dease and Mrs Leigh-White for a carved tray and to Mrs and Miss Beatty for the brass plate on the door.

Annual Report, 1936

———

Unexpectedly, the lease was not renewed the following November, and a new premises had to be found. A new premises, at 28 South Frederick Street, was found, and headquarters moved there in November 1936. Guides would hold the lease on that property for eleven years, until they moved to 16 St Stephen's Green in 1947.

Nineteen thirty-five also saw the IFSGG begin to supply its members with material 'made in our own country', which helped reduce costs. Uniforms and badges were now manufactured in Ireland. At Christmas that year, Dublin Guides and Rangers collected toys, books, sweets, fruit and games to hand out around the city. The act of delivering the gifts became known as the 'Stocking Trail'. The trail extended over forty companies from Kilternan to Malahide, and the girls involved filled 306 stockings and distributed them at the St John's Ambulance Association welfare dining rooms to poor families. The filling and distribution of stockings became known as 'the Christmas Stocking Trail' and was for many years an important event for Dublin units.

A popular game called Captainball began in units in the 1930s. Captainball is a non-contact team game which is often played in Guide

Guides playing Captainball at camp in the early 1970s.

units. There are seven players on each team, each of whom attempts to get the ball back to their captain. The game is known and loved by generations of Girl Guides. International matches were held between Belfast and Dublin units, and even Trefoil Guild (an organisation made up of leaders who are no longer active in units but wish to stay involved in Guiding); the tournament continued for decades. The game itself is accessible to everyone, regardless of their age or level of fitness. It encourages teamwork, competition and dexterity. What better expression of the Guide spirit could there be?

Due to the fact that the Irish Free State Guides still took much of its programme from the UK Girl Guides, it was felt that more attention should be paid to the Irish language and customs within the programme of the new association. In 1935, an Irish Language and Arts Committee was set up, to act in an advisory capacity to the executive committee on Irish matters. It began by creating a syllabus for Guides and Rangers which included Irish dancing, Irish music, history, cooking, embroidery and legend.

The international aspect of Guiding continued to grow. This was acknowledged by Lady Powerscourt in the 1936 annual report:

Opposite: Guides handing out gifts as part of the Stocking Trail in the 1960s.

I am glad that so many of our Guides have been able to get abroad this year; Sweden, Denmark, Holland, Belgium, England and Switzerland have all welcomed us as guests, and we in turn have welcomed here Guides from Sweden, Holland, England,

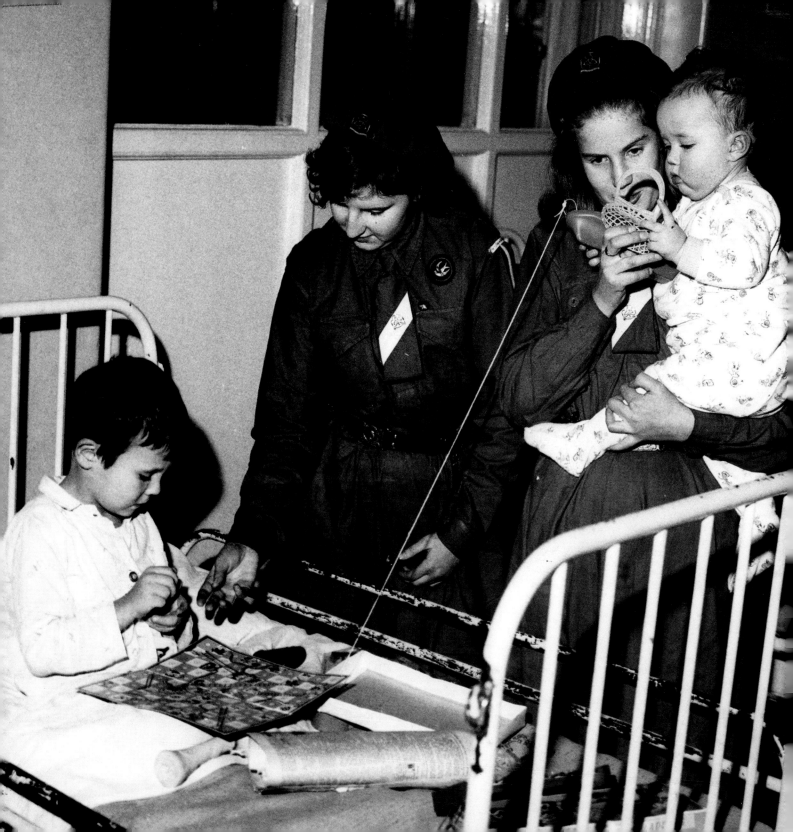

Mrs Gossett, the designer of The Chief Commissioner's Banner.

Wales and Scotland. It is this opportunity for personal contact, the interchange of thought, of interest and enjoyment, which makes World Guiding of such immense value.

———ᴠᴠᴠ———

To be able to afford these international adventures, the association realised that fund-raising would have to become part of their long-term plans. A gift sale was held in Powerscourt, which raised £320. There was a slight increase in company numbers in 1936 'but owing to several severe cases of illness, and to an epidemic of matrimony among [our] Guiders, several companies have been unable to hold regular meetings'. Despite this, there were 2,918 enrolled members on the books at this time. The main problem for units was still a lack of leaders, but this did not stop some of the smaller counties producing young women to be proud of:

The Eadestown Guides in County Kildare have only had occasional meetings during the long illness of their Captain. But their company is to be congratulated on a good contribution to public service. One of the patrol leaders, hearing through her Guider, two years ago, of the new scheme for slum playgrounds under the Civic Institute of the

Dublin Corporation, offered herself for training and is now in charge of a playground for six hundred children at Cabra; an excellent outcome of her Guide training in the use of games in education.

Annual Report, 1936

In Sligo and Wexford, a scheme for providing Guides with gardens, with competitions for the best designs, proved a great success. Cork formed a 'Lone Group' which consisted of the 'survivors' of companies which were no longer active. The first meeting of this group took the form of a campfire on Thinking Day, 1936. In 1937, another new group was started for women who were still interested in Guiding but were not active members. They became known as 'Old Guides'.

It was planned to hold the world conference in Ireland in 1937 but 'owing to the adverse rate of exchange and the great expense involved by the long journey to Ireland the World Committee felt it necessary to ask the members whether it would not be wise to postpone holding the world conference here in the Irish Free State next year' (Letter from Lady Powerscourt to the Executive Committee of The Irish Free State Girl Guides, October 1937). In a letter from Dame Katherine Furse, director of the world bureau, it was mentioned that the Irish Girl Guides should have the same number of representatives at the world conference as they would have had if it had gone ahead in Ireland, as it 'is through no fault of theirs that the conference is not meeting in Ireland'. The world conference would not return to Ireland until 1999.

On 12 May 1937, all parts of the British Empire were preparing for the coronation of King George VI and Queen Elizabeth. A coronation camp was held in Chigwell and the Irish Guides (as a dominion) were invited to send ten Guides.

Previous:
*Scots Church
Rangers on a
hillside in
Glencullen.*

On the day of the coronation, the new king and queen travelled to Westminster Abbey, and along the route Scouts greeted each group in the procession, including the marching Guides. Many of the visitors viewed the procession from Constitution Hill, and one reported his experiences in the *Scouter* (a magazine covering all aspects of Scouting). He commented that the watching Scouts did a great deal of singing: as each contingent of the procession came by, they sang an appropriate tune. The

Royal Navy, for example, were met with 'Popeye the Sailorman', and the police with 'John Peel'. The correspondent wrote: 'because a Scout is courteous, we greeted the Girl Guides with "Why were they born so beautiful?"'

A new concept was introduced in 1937: Touring Guiders. These Guiders would visit companies in any county at the request of commissioners. It was felt that this would greatly help companies whose Guiders were unable to get much training, and would also keep Headquarters in touch with Guiding throughout the country. These Guiders underwent extensive training before visiting others around the country.

In 1938, the IFSGG underwent another name change, to reflect the political situation following the 1937 referendum. The Irish people had ratified a new constitution in which the Irish Free State was renamed, simply, 'Ireland', or 'Éire'. The association would enter the turbulent times of the Second World War as 'The Irish Girl Guides'.

Collecting wood and water at camp in 1935.

Opposite: *Agnes Baden-Powell at Chigwell Row Camp in 1937.*

CHAPTER 4

The Irish Girl Guides and the Second World War

As political borders changed, so did the borders of the Girl Guide movement worldwide. The Irish Free State Girl Guides recognised this fact in March 1938 when they voted to change their name from the Irish Free State Girl Guides to the simpler The Irish Girl Guides (this has remained unchanged with the exception of dropping the capital 'T' in 2009). Lady Powerscourt noted this change in her yearly submission to the Annual Review:

> An important item which had to be done during 1938 was our change of name. We had got so used to the 'Irish Free State Girl Guides' that we said goodbye to them with regret, but I know that 'The Irish Girl Guides', though changed in name, will lose nothing in efficiency and principle.

Guides at church parade at St Patrick's Cathedral in 1943.

Simplicity was the order of the day. At the same conference in March 1938, it was decided to change the Promise from 'I promise on my honour to do my duty to

Registration Cerificate of the 2nd Wicklow Company, 1939.

God, my country and the Oireachtas and to help other people . . . ' to the slightly more straightforward 'I promise on my honour to do my duty to God and my country . . . '. This, it was felt, would be much easier for Brownies to learn. At the conference, it was also decided to stock a library at Headquarters; books could be borrowed at a rate of two pence a fortnight. The library was for the use of commissioners, Guiders and Rangers. A new official uniform was introduced; it consisted of a dress in cotton or wool made of the official Guide Blue and cut to the pattern provided by Headquarters. Rangers and Guides could wear either brown or black shoes and stockings, provided the entire unit wore the same colour. The Guide badge with the Celtic knot and trefoil was also seen for the first time. The trefoil is an international symbol of Guiding and most member countries have some form of it as part of their national symbol. The three trefoil leaves represent the three parts of the Guide Promise: 'To serve God and my country, to help people at all times and to obey the Girl Guide Law'. The addition of the Celtic knot made the trefoil uniquely Irish.

Also in 1938, the Irish Girl Guides were presented with an Irish harp by Miss Carrie Townsend, who offered to teach one of the members to play it. It was noted in a letter from Eileen Beatty to all Captains and Brown Owls that:

> The Irish harp is, as you know, mainly used for accompanying songs, and we feel that it would be delightful for camp fires, both at home and at International camps.

The girl who took up the offer, Debra Metcalf, went on to play the harp at the Pax Ting camp in Hungary. The harp itself, unfortunately, does not exist any more, and no one is sure what happened to it; in the 1950s, it was still being mentioned in *Trefoil News* and was available to play in Headquarters. Arethusa Leigh-White, who had been involved with Irish Guiding for many years and had served as commissioner for Cork, deputy chief commissioner and international commissioner, moved from Irish Guiding to director of the world bureau in London (a position she held until 1947). When leaving, she noted in the annual report that:

> there is a quality in Guiding which does surmount [difficulties and tasks], and my own firm conviction is, no matter what trials, difficulties and even reverses we may have to face even yet, the true Guide Spirit will carry us through, and what is more, will, by the strength of its very disinterestedness, bring influence to bear upon the bigger issues which are bewildering the world today. What is required of each one of us, whether it be at home or abroad, is that our own individual effort should move along the lines of all that is intended by the Promise and Law of Guiding, and so along the path of a greater faith, a greater understanding and a greater good for the benefit of all mankind. A Guide is a sister to every other Guide *but* she is also a *friend to all*.

In 1939, a group of twenty-six girls went to an International Camp at Godolla near Budapest, Hungary, called Pax Ting – a name gathered from different languages which, roughly translated, means 'peace gathering' or 'peace

Overleaf: The Irish delegation at Pax Ting 1939.

parliament'. Each contingent brought their own equipment. The journey was arduous: the Irish group travelled to London, where they stayed for a night, followed by two nights and a day travelling by train from Ostend. The girls who attended the camp noted that 'a tribute must be paid to the courage of the Hungarian Guides, who persisted with their plans for this Peace Gathering through continued rumours of unrest and war'. The camp ended on 8 August; Germany invaded Poland on 1 September.

As the great powers of Europe moved inexorably towards war, Ireland declared a state of emergency in September 1939. The war years were particularly busy for the Irish Girl Guides. Young women in particular found that the war changed their lives dramatically. Many worked in jobs which had traditionally been filled by men. Although Ireland remained neutral, many women served in the armed forces and other services.

Where the previous two decades had been characterised by tending to the growth and development of Guiding in Ireland, the war years had an entirely different character. The annual report of 1939 expressed the Guiding movement's sympathies with those caught up in the conflict:

> Our thoughts and sympathies are with . . . those other Guides who are suffering such hardships in lands less fortunate than our own. We can only hope and pray for happier times . . . [and] remember the contacts with our sister Guides in many lands, made in that spirit of friendship which, through all the isolation of wartime conditions, unites us throughout the Guide movement.
>
> Ethel Moore, *International Commissioner*, 1939

Throughout German-occupied Europe, many Guide and Scout organisations were suppressed and forced to meet clandestinely. The IGG attempted as much as possible to continue with regular activities and training, but were always willing to help with the war effort in any way needed. Before the outbreak of war, the chief commissioner had written to the government offering the services of the adult members of the IGG in the event of war breaking out:

> Dear Mr de Valera,
>
> For some time past, the Executive Committee of the Irish Girl Guides has been considering how best our organisation could be of use in the event of an international crisis affecting our country.
>
> We have about seven hundred adult members, and hundreds of past members, who we feel sure would help if the necessity arose.
>
> With our training, we might, as an organisation, be of use in such work as the evacuation of women and children, the management of a refugee hostel, ARP work among women and children, etc.
>
> We therefore offer the services of our adult members to the government and, if called upon, will do all in our power to carry out any work entrusted to us to the best of our ability. We also are prepared

Eileen Beatty and Eamon de Valera examining gas masks in 1939.

to train for any branch of work if required.

Yours truly,

(Viscountess) Powerscourt

Chief Commissioner

—◠◡◠—

The government realised the worth of a well-organised, socially minded group of volunteers, and in September 1939 the Irish Girl Guides were asked by Dublin Corporation if they could provide volunteers to help collect civilian gas masks. In the space of a single weekend, around 150 volunteers were produced for training. In August 1940, they were asked to help with the assembly of those masks; they worked alongside the Boy Scouts, Catholic Boy Scouts of Ireland, the Boys' Brigade and the Catholic Girl Guides of the Diocese of Dublin. Four hundred thousand units were made, and the Guides were asked to take charge in each depot.

In that period, Guides were also involved in preparing and packing aid packages to be sent to Poland and Romania, while the 1st East Cork (Cobh) Company knitted woollen scarves and other garments for distribution to crews of ships wrecked off the Cork coast (a number of cargo ships were sunk off the coast of Ireland during the war). With the inevitable shortages that war brings, Guides decided to learn to cultivate their gardens; as part of this, the IGG held competitions to identify the best gardeners.

Headquarters was cleared of all superfluous furniture, equipment, carpets, curtains and so on, and turned into a depot for making dressings for the Irish Red Cross Emergency Hospitals Supply Depot; Guiders, Rangers and Senior Guides worked there every afternoon and evening. Because the hospitals were running out of cotton wool, the dressings were made from sphagnum moss, collected by Girl Guides. With the strain of war taking its toll, the entire Scouting and Guiding movement had barely time to mourn the death, in 1941, in Kenya, of their founder and Chief Scout of the World, Lord Baden-Powell. In Ireland, a special service was held in St Patrick's Cathedral, a Benediction was said at the Irish Lourdes in Inchicore, and a service was held at the synagogue on Adelaide Road. Lord Baden-Powell found time in his final days to send one last message 'to the Girl Guides of the World'. It reads like the final message of a father to his children. Just as many Guides and Scouts saw him as a father figure, he saw them as his children:

My dear Guides,

This is just a farewell note to you. It is just to remind you, when I have passed on, that your business in life is to be happy and to make others happy. That sounds comfortable and easy, doesn't it? You begin making other people happy by doing good turns to them. You need to worry about making yourselves happy, as you will very soon find that comes by itself, when you make other people happy. Later on, when you have a home of your own by making it a bright and cheery one, you will make your husband a happy man. . . . It may mean hard work for you, but will bring its reward; if you keep your children healthy, clean and busy, they will be happy. Happy children love their parents. There is nothing can give you greater joy than a loving child.

I am sure God means us to be happy in this life. He has given us a world to live in that is full of beauties and wonders, and He has given

Lord and Lady Baden-Powell in 1932. (Copyright Girlguiding UK)

us not only eyes to see them but minds to understand them if we only have the sense to look at them in that light. We can enjoy bright sunshine and glorious views. We can see the beauty in the flowers. We can watch with wonder how the seed produces the young plant which grows to a flower which in its turn will replace other flowers as they die off. For, though plants, like people, die, their race does not die away, but new ones are born, and grow up to carry on the Creator's plan.

So, do you see, you are the chosen servants of God in two ways: first to carry on the race, to bring children into the world to replace the men and women who pass away; secondly, to bring happiness into the world by making happy homes and by being yourselves good, cheery comrades for your husbands and children. That is where you as Guides especially come in: by taking an interest in your husband's work and aspirations, you can also help him with your sympathy and suggestions and so be a Guide to him. Also, by strengthening and training the minds and characters of your children, you will be giving them a better use and enjoyment of life.

Unpacking gear at camp in the 1930s.

By giving out love and happiness in this way you will gain for yourselves the return love of husband and children, and there is nothing better in this world. You will find that Heaven is not the kind of happiness somewhere up in the skies after you are dead, but right here and now in this world in your own home.

So *Guide* others to happiness and you will bring happiness to yourselves, and by doing this you will be doing what God wants of you.

God be with you.

—⁓—

His devoted wife Olave said in her diary: 'He looked so sweet and perfect in death as he was in life - utterly, utterly noble and good and dear and wonderful, great and faultless.'

Meanwhile, in Ireland, in a bid to cling to normality, not all non-emergency activities were suspended, but all were tinged in some way by the war effort. For example, the 1941 Exhibition of Guide Homecrafts and Handicrafts – held at the Mansion House on 3 April – was concerned not so much with fine handiwork but with the thrift and clever use of waste material on show. Overall, the war kept Guides on both sides of the border busy. When Guides in Belfast were affected by bombing by German planes, Irish Girl Guides raised £70, which they sent to alleviate any losses which were experienced by them. There was no caveat attached to the money and it could be used as seen fit by the local leaders.

In 1943, a decision was taken – albeit much delayed by the war – at the Commissioners' Conference and Council Meeting that there should be a memorial in the country to Lord Baden-Powell. The commissioners decided that it should take the form of a cottage, which would be a centre for outdoor Guiding. Even then, the war impinged: it was decided that part of the funds raised for the cottage – through the hard work of individual members saving and working to earn the money – should be used for relief work amongst children in Europe. Girl Guides wrote to Olave Baden-Powell to inform her of their decision. She wrote back, saying:

> I do hope that all your Companies and Packs are enjoying their work
> and are thrilled with this plan of making a lovely Guide House of your
> own, which, as you say, is just what our beloved Founder would have

liked you to do. It will be so helpful and inspiring to have a centre, from which all Guides can carry away new ideas, new enthusiasm, and new determination to make their share of Guiding the best ever. I send you all my best wishes in your great endeavour.

—◦◦◦—

In spite of the war, the Irish Girl Guides were determined to continue striving, and May 1943 saw the first publication of *Trefoil News*, the association's new bi-monthly magazine. *Trefoil News* is now a monthly publication received by all adult and young leaders every month from September to June. In a letter thanking Eileen Beatty for sending her a copy of the first publication, Lady Baden-Powell noted that it was splendid that the Guides:

> have now got their own news-sheet, to help spread knowledge of Guiding in all its different forms, to bring all Guides all over Eire in touch with one another and to encourage everyone in their share of the great game that we are all playing together all the world over.
>
> 2 August 1943

—◦◦◦—

The first edition of *Trefoil News* began with a discussion of the progress on the memorial to Lord Baden-Powell and went on to explain to Guiders that this was their magazine and would rely on their contributions – particularly in the absence of annual reports (which were not produced during the war).

The first volume of Trefoil News, *May 1943.*

Trefoil News

No. 1   THE IRISH GIRL GUIDES   May 1943

Our Memorial to the Chief

THIS PORTRAIT reminds many of us of our Chief, Lord Baden-Powell of Gilwell, who died in January, 1941, and was founder of the Boy Scout and Girl Guide Movements. It reminds us of his young eyes and his gallant figure and the thrill we once had hearing him speak from some platform about Guiding. But what about all the Guides who will never see him—and the Brownies and Rangers and Guiders also less fortunate. They want to remember and be reminded of him, too, and not forget his fine enthusiasm and to say thank-you to him in some way he would have liked.

So this first number of TREFOIL NEWS is opening with a discussion about our special memorial to him in Eire. Much has already been done. It was decided at the Commissioners' Conference and approved by Council that part of the money collected should go to an international fund, and the rest to the buying or building of a stone house, a kind of white-washed Irish Adelboden, in our own mountains or overlooking the Irish Sea or the green fields. Here we could hurry away at week-ends or take our Companies or Packs in the summer, and we could invite and put up visiting Guides and Guiders from other countries. On the grass outside it we could have a flag-pole for our own Irish Girl Guides' Flag, and over the door memorial lettering and possibly a head and shoulders plaque of the Chief. It would be a centre for camping, and have all the advantages of a camp, a place for practising real woodcraft and tracking and for making friends with all the living things of the woodland or shore, for mapping and stalking and cooking and camouflage unrestricted by the four walls of a hall. Above all it would be a house where Guides could meet and make friends and re-catch from each other the fun of Guiding. Round its open turf fire we would gather in the evenings to warm ourselves (and probably dry our stockings, since it will be in Ireland), to talk and have camp-fire with the flame-light catching the white of the crockery on the dresser and flickering over the circle of uniforms and faces. But, alas the house isn't bought yet!

Whether it is our ideal—built on two or so acres of wood and grass on a conspicuous site, with room for twenty to sleep indoors and more out and a lovely big living-room —or something less, depends on how much money is contributed to our Memorial Fund.

You will want to start collecting at once, but, before you begin, we advise you to discuss it with your Guiding neighbours, so that not only existing Companies but Old Guides, Lones, past Guiders and those who now or in the past have been interested in Guiding may be included in a scheme for your district, and yet the same people not asked twice. We are sure you will be full of ideas for concerts, fetes, sales, etc., to raise money, but ask you to avoid raffles. Subscriptions should be sent to the Honorary Treasurer, Memorial Fund, the Irish Girl Guides Headquarters, 28 South Frederick Street, Dublin. December 1st is fixed as a preliminary closing date when the Treasurer will add up the contributions, and the fund will close finally on March 31st, 1944, giving us—if all goes well, time to have the Memorial Lodge ready for use in the Summer, 1944.

We hope you will agree that such a house will, by attracting us out to the wilds and encouraging us to be better campers and nature-lovers, be the most fitting memorial to our Chief who was a person for out-of-doors and adventures from the beginning to the end of his life. Please send extra ideas for it as well as contributions. We don't yet know where it will be, but we picture it having a path or a lane or an avenue up to it. Imagine at the foot of this an eager Irish Girl Guide, enrolled in 1943 and full of excitement at being a Guide, longing to climb up. Every step she takes will be £1. We think the path may have 2,000 steps, how many will your Company or Pack help her to take?

Trefoil News featured short stories, news on national events, camping tips, company news, changes in uniform, and changes in programme. One of the first articles to be published concerned the standards which should be upheld at camp, including the fact that no girl could be seen in public without a proper uniform on:

> As the time for camping approaches, I should like to appeal to Guiders and Commandants of camps to please see that their Guides are clean and tidy when going out of camp – hats and ties should be worn and Guide blue socks or stockings. Remember it is not only your own Company's or camp's reputation that is at stake, it is the whole Guide Movement's – don't let it down please.
>
> Adela Guise Brown, Head of Camping, *Trefoil News*, 1943

As the tide of the war turned in the Allies' favour, the world bureau began to make contact with the many national organisations which had been effectively cut off from them during the war. The Bureau had decided that once hostilities were over, teams of Guiders would be sent to war-torn areas of Europe to restart and encourage Guiding wherever it could be found. These teams went through tough training in order to be able to deal with the rough and sometimes dangerous terrain they would have to cross. This training was initiated by the Guide International Service, which was explicitly set up to bring relief and rehabilitation to Guiding in Europe. Well trained and with hearts full of the Guiding Spirit, Guiders from Ireland willingly went forth to help their sister Guides in whatever way they could.

CHAPTER 5

Guiding in Post-war Ireland

As part of post-war activities, and in an attempt to reinvigorate Guiding in war-torn Europe, many relief-based projects were planned. Money from the fund which was to be used for the memorial cottage for Baden-Powell was redirected to what was termed 'international aid'. In 1945, money was sent to Switzerland for refugee children; to Sweden, to buy food and footwear for Norwegian children; and to France, Belgium, Luxembourg, the Netherlands and the Polish Guides in France to buy food for children.

Closer to home, a camp was planned at St Columba's College, Rathfarnham, for Dutch and French Guides who had experienced difficult times during the war. The plane carrying the French Guides got lost en route to Ireland and crashed in Wicklow on 12 August 1946. Luckily there were no fatalities, but most of the visitors spent their time in Ireland in hospital. The crash made the national newspapers and was the talk of the camp. On 13 August, the *Irish Times* reported:

Malahide Sea Rangers posing in their new uniforms in 1958.

The French plane that crashed in Wicklow in 1946.

A French plane, bringing twenty-three French Girl Guides to Dublin to spend a holiday with the Irish Girl Guides, crashed on Djouce mountain, in Wicklow, at 1.30 yesterday afternoon. The wreckage was not found until shortly before midnight. Many of the girls were injured, some seriously, and all were suffering from the effects of eleven hours' exposure on the mountain in torrential floods and a fifty-miles-an-hour gale.

In 1998, fourteen survivors returned to Ireland to revisit the scene of the crash, to visit the two hospitals they had stayed in, and to meet the people who had been involved in their rescue and subsequent recovery. In 2005, Suzanne Barnes published a book entitled *When Our Plane Hit the Mountain*; many of the survivors again returned to Ireland for the launch.

Because of travel restrictions during the war, the Chief Guide, Olave Baden-Powell, had been somewhat cut off from the Guiding world during the war. Her first visit to Ireland after peace had been declared was in 1946. She stayed for ten days, during which time she visited Cork, Sligo, Dundalk, Waterford, Bray and Dublin. The 1946 annual review stated:

> Wherever she went she was greeted with the greatest enthusiasm, and her smile, her friendliness and her selfless devotion to Guiding left a very deep impression here. She found time for everything and for everyone, from the chief commissioner to the wee-est brownie, including a public meeting at the Mansion House, Dublin.

Programme from Lady Baden-Powell's visit to Cork in 1946.

Following her visit, Lady Baden-Powell wrote in a letter to Eileen Beatty:

> It has been such a real pleasure to visit you again after this long time, and I have so much appreciated all that was done in arranging the various meetings and rallies. I feel confident that even though these

Overleaf: A group at the camp at St Columba's College in 1946.

will have given people a lot of extra work, and cost time and effort (and money!), they will have stimulated fresh enthusiasm, and given all the Guides, as well as their leaders, a new zest for their activities. I have indeed been pleased and impressed by much that I have seen and heard.

In December 1946, the chief commissioner, Lady Sybil Powerscourt, died suddenly. She had been involved with Irish Guiding since its introduction to Ireland in 1911 and was sadly missed by her friends and colleagues. Eileen Beatty wrote at the time:

Looking back through the years, we remember her in innumerable happy ways, her interest in all details of our work, her attendance at meetings of the Executive Committee and General Council, and her friendship and help in either joy or sorrow. . . . In the years that lie ahead there will be other chief commissioners, but there will always be in our hearts the very happy memory of one who was our first chief commissioner.

'Those were the days', *Trefoil News*

Her position as chief commissioner was assumed by her daughter-in-law, Lady Sheila Powerscourt. In 1947, the Irish Girl Guides presented a Ford V8 van, 'Arethusa', to the world bureau for the 'encouragement of Guiding wherever it has sprung up after the war and needs help'. On one side of the van were the words 'Presented to the World Association of Girl Guides and Girl Scouts by the

Irish Girl Guides in memory of the Founder'. In the spring of 1947, Estelle Moore, from Cork, had been accepted as part of the international team sent by the world bureau to restart Guiding in Austria. The team, who were determined to revive Guiding in Europe, travelled in 'Arethusa' and worked with children in displaced persons' camps. Estelle sent bulletins home so that her fellow Guides could read about the work she and her team were undertaking. In her first bulletin, in May 1947, she said:

Arethusa in 1947.

We have spent our first night 'on board', and very snug and peaceful it has been. . . . Over the hatch just above my bunk is a long shelf with a deep ledge, stretching the width of the vehicle. This is our larder, a most important spot . . . . The starboard side and all available corners are pretty well filled with all the camping and training gear which we are taking to Austria. . . . Yesterday we drove through glorious country . . . . This morning we hope to cross into Switzerland at Basle and reach Zurich by the afternoon. Then on Monday or Tuesday we shall forge ahead – Austria at last. To go back a little . . . Arethusa was christened by Mrs Leigh-White standing outside the world bureau, and 'Our Ark' . . . is a great big, sleek grey van, a Ford V8 with double wheels aft and the solid chassis we'll need for the Austrian roads. . . . Now are you all feeling proud and glad of every bit of hard work that went into those sales and all the other ways by which the money was raised? And do you really realise that I'm here representing you, your envoy to the Austrian and Displaced Persons' Guides, not to mention all those who hail us along our route, when they see the World Trefoil. . . . We are going to encourage Guiding wherever it has sprung up after the war and needs help, but not to start new branches of the movement. Arethusa will carry us to all the centres where little or big groups of Guides are just longing for training and contact with our great World Sisterhood.

—⚬∿⚬—

Camping and outdoor activities continued to be central to the Guide programme. Today, lightweight camping is greatly aided by lightweight materials: many essential items can be packed away in small rucksacks and even food can be designed to be lightweight. Although equipment was not quite as 'light' in 1949, there were still ways of keeping gear lightweight and easy to carry. In 1948, *Trefoil News* suggested:

Girls working hard at camp.

I always feel that our bedding is the heaviest part of our personal camp equipment, so here are a few ideas on warmth without weight. You all know how beautifully warm yet light a Shetland shawl is, yet when you examine it, it is all holes! You see, it is all the air entangled in the meshes that makes the shawl warm in use. Why not knit yourself a sleeping blanket? Add an extra pair of socks and a cardigan or shawl to come down over your hips, and you will have greatly increased the warmth. Do you know that the tighter you roll your clothes, the less they are creased? So make yourself some bags of plastic just big enough to hold your extras. The tip for sewing plastic is either to Vaseline the needle or rub French chalk on both sides of the plastic.

Babies muslin 'nappies' make grand lightweight towels and also dry quickly. A bag made of curtain

IRISH GIRL GUIDE CHOIR -(DUBLIN AREA.)

WINNERS LADIES' CHOIRS - FEIS CEOIL 1949.

N.BARR. P.DORMER. D.ROWE. A.GALWAY. H.CROSS. I.INGLIS. J.ALLBUTT.
M.GREENE. D.JOHNSTON. V.JOHNSTON. D.BRADBURY. E.LEACH. L.ALLMAN. B.JACKSON. O.HASLAM.
E.SMITH. A.DUMBLETON. E.FENNEL. MRS O SMITH. P.HAZLETT. L.DUMBLETON. D.WALSH.

net and an extra pocket outside for your soap give your facecloth, toothbrush and soap a chance to dry out during the day. You will have no more horrid soft slimy soap if you do this.

The Irish Girl Guide Choir (Dublin Area) 1949.

Ireland had suffered economically during the war, due to the cutting off of trade routes from Ireland; attacks on Irish ships and a lack of access to foreign boats which had always been used by Irish companies (twenty Merchant Irish ships were sunk in the course of the war resulting in the loss of 138 lives). As the world began to recover from the effects of the Second World War and Ireland battled to rebuild its economy, travel became easier and life began to return to normal. As the association rolled into its fifth decade, Guiding continued to enjoy a strong place in Irish society.

Among the most exciting developments for Irish Guiding in the 1950s was the opening of a National Memorial Cottage in Enniskerry. The January 1950 edition of *Trefoil News* contained an invitation to each county to choose two Guides to stay in the cottage for the weekend immediately after the official opening on 1 July. Booking forms were sent out with the March edition: the charges were fixed at one shilling and sixpence per person per night Monday to Friday, two shillings for Saturday and Sunday nights, and ten shillings and sixpence per person for a full week.

Plans for the cottage had begun in 1943, when it was decided by the executive committee to set up a Baden-Powell memorial fund with a view ultimately to providing a cottage as a home for Guides in Ireland. Subscriptions were sent in from all over the country, and by the end of 1944, £1,686.17.5 had been raised. However, as we have seen, it was agreed in 1945

Sea Rangers parading in Lansdowne Road in 1952.

I hope, said young Jil, the girl guide,

That good care they will take to provide

In our cottage quite small,

ODEAREST *S for all,*

Then we'll take every test in our stride.

TRADE ENQUIRIES TO:

O'DEA & CO., LTD. WOLFE TONE HOUSE, DUBLIN.

to use part of the funds to help with various relief funds in the aftermath of the war. Subscriptions were sent to the Irish Red Cross (which was also involved in the war effort), the World Association of Girl Guides and the B.P. Memorial fund in Great Britain and about £500 was given towards the expenses of the camp in St Columba's College, Rathfarnham.

By 1949, things had settled down somewhat, and the original plan to build a cottage was reinstated. A site was chosen in Enniskerry on the lands of Lord Powerscourt, who gave the site on a 150-year lease at a nominal ground rent of £1 a year. The site was described by Eileen Beatty as having 'everything we want. It is almost too good to be true'. The plans featured a kitchen, a large dormitory, a Guiders' dormitory, a bathroom, toilets and a large common room. A list of the required fixtures and fittings was sent to all members of the organisation, and gifts were forwarded to furnish the cottage. In addition, all ranks were asked to make knitted squares for blankets for the bunks; most of them were sent in complete with the name of the Pack or Company knitted in the centre square. The Jewish Rovers had offered to help: they were asked to build a wooden hut in the grounds to house fuel and bicycles. The plaque over the fireplace in the common room reads:

The Cottage was built by the Irish Girl Guides in memory of Lord Baden-Powell, Founder of Scouting and Guiding, 1950.

—⟋⟋⟍—

Irene Kinley receiving her medal from Lady Baden-Powell.

The cottage was officially opened in July 1950. Lady Baden-Powell was in attendance, along with 1,500 Guides. She spent the morning of the ceremony visiting the Brownies and Guides who had gathered at the cottage. One proud Brownie, Freda Keady from Kilternan, noted recently:

> my biggest moment was when I was at the official opening of the National Cottage in Enniskerry and meeting Lady Baden Powell. I will never forget how the heavens opened with a downpour shortly after.

—⟋⟋⟍—

Lady Baden-Powell presented a medal for gallantry to a Brownie, Irene Kinley, aged nine, who had pulled her baby sister out of a fire and then extinguished her flaming clothing with her hands.

After lunch, Lady Sheila Powerscourt and General Mulcahy, the Minister for Education, gave speeches. Lady Baden-Powell then stood up to address the waiting Brownies, Guides and dignitaries. She read a telegram from the World Association in London, bringing greetings from 2,500,000 Guides throughout the world. Lady Baden-Powell was very taken with the cottage, remarking:

> Here you will find a home for the Guides of Ireland, and I would like to offer my congratulations to all who contributed to the building of this cottage.

Opposite: An ad for a fundraising sale in aid of the Memorial Cottage 1949.

—✤—

She then proceeded to the hall door, pressed the latch, and found inside a Guard of Honour of Brownies and a Guide choir, who sang 'Bless This House'. In a letter of thanks to Doris Findlater (the first warden of the Cottage), she wrote:

> I just can't get over the charm of that cottage and the fact that you have raised the funds, and built and equipped it, and made it so utterly delightful. I do so rejoice with and for you, at the success of your great endeavour, and I am quite sure that the cottage is going to be the greatest boon and delight to Guides and Guiders, as well as a very real asset for the association.
>
> You see, I feel very strongly, and I expect that you do too, that ownership of a property puts us on a higher footing, and gives us greater status! Now Ireland ranks with all other countries, and states, and places, that have their own Guide Houses, and I feel, therefore, proud with you – and happy – that you have got your cottage now in being. And what a *sweet* cottage it is too!

—✤—

The opening of the cottage was reported in the *Irish Independent* on 3 July 1950:

> The Baden-Powell Memorial Cottage erected by the Irish Girl Guides was opened by Lady Baden-Powell, World Chief Guide.
>
> The cottage is situated in County Wicklow on the Tinnahinch Road between Enniskerry and Powerscourt. The site was given to the Guides by Lord Powerscourt.

Over 1,500 members of the movement were present at the opening ceremony, and they came from Dublin, Carlow, Cork, Donegal, Kildare, Limerick, Louth, Monaghan, Sligo, Waterford, Wexford and Wicklow. Addressing the Guides, Lady Baden-Powell said the cottage gave the Irish organisation a home.

General Mulcahy, Minister for Education, said it was a delight to him to see Guides from all over Ireland brought together in the spirit of true Christian comradeship. Boy Scouts and Girl Guides had often a wider general training than university students.

Before leaving, General Mulcahy presented Lady Powerscourt with two books for the cottage library – a book on Dublin and *The Irish Traditions* by Robin Flower.

Lady Powerscourt, chief commissioner, said the cottage, which would accommodate twenty-two people, would be used for training and recreation. The ground on which the cottage stood would be used for camping.

The cottage continues to be part of Irish Guiding, although it has undergone some changes. In 1954, electricity was introduced. In 1959, the kitchen was extended. For the Silver Jubilee in 1961, ten pine trees and sixty privet hedges were planted. In 1979, it was decided that, rather than continue to pay rent to the Powerscourt estate, the Guides should buy the freehold. Another extension was begun in 1981, to add more dormitory accommodation, and toilets and washing facilities; this extension was opened in 1982. In 1991, the woodshed was

burnt to the ground, so in 1992 a concrete shed was constructed. Also in 1992, the Slazenger family (the owners of the Powerscourt estate) provided additional land to be used for cars and coach turning and parking. Though there have been cosmetic changes to the cottage, it retains at its core the idea of being a gathering place for the Irish Girl Guides, and a place where they can all feel at home.

The Trefoil Guild, an association for members who have retired but still wish to be part of the Guide community, was founded in 1953. The Guild invariably helps out with events and special occasions. They also have guest speakers, outings and meetings, and were very active in the annual captainball tournaments. They are always happy to roll up their sleeves and tackle any job to which they can make a contribution.

In 1957, more than 260 Irish Guides attended camps in Britain, Norway, Switzerland and Northern Ireland to celebrate the centenary of the birth of Lord Baden-Powell. The same year, the annual Christmas stocking trail continued, with 676 stockings and copious amounts of toys and books donated. As part of the stocking trail, Guides and Brownies were encouraged to pack stockings with items such as toys, sweets, fruit, books, pencils and games. They also collected donations of food and clothes. Stockings were delivered to the Civics Institute of Ireland; the Children's Hospital, Harcourt Street; the Children's Hospital, Temple Street; the Dublin Fever Hospital, Cherry Orchard, Clondalkin; St Patrick's Nurses' Home, St Stephen's Green; Little Sisters of the Assumption, Camden Street; St John's Orphanage, Sandymount; and Lakelands Industrial School, Sandymount.

Lady Sheila Powerscourt resigned as chief commissioner in 1957 owing to ill health, and Eileen Beatty became chief commissioner. Eileen Beatty was a long-standing member of the organisation and had served in a number of roles,

Previous: *A group of Gold Cord Guides from Cork with an impressive collection of badges.*

Opposite: *Two Cadets in 1959.*

including international commissioner. She was also on the world committee and chaired the WAGGGS finance committee. She was the first chief commissioner to come from outside the Powerscourt family and remained in the position until 1970, when she became president of the IGG.

Nineteen fifty-seven was a Jubilee year for the Scouts: a celebration was held in St Patrick's Cathedral, with 3,500 Scouts and Guides present. The colours of all the Scout and Guide companies present were paraded through the cathedral and were laid in the Lady Chapel during the service; the service ended with a rendition of 'Taps'.

Until 1958, the IGG had been using proficiency-badge books issued by the Girl Guide Association (GGA) (now Girlguiding UK). There were references to Ireland in these books (with one section being headed 'How to write to the Archbishop of Dublin'). The GGA book continued to be used in Ireland, with an insert stuck on the inside cover giving Ireland-specific material, including the Irish Guide Law and Promise. In the early 1950s, the IGG began work on their own publication, *The Guide Branch Book of Tests, Proficiency Badges etc!*; this book was issued in 1958. The new book included seven Irish badges, including 'Irish Language' and 'Irish Dancing'. The book remained the template for subsequent editions until the 1980s.

The badges were constantly evolving to reflect the world in which the girls lived. For example, the first badge in the 1958 book is 'Aircraft': the Guide needed to be able to identify bombers, fighters, flying boats, seaplanes and troop carriers, as well as civil passenger-carrying aircraft.

Guides are always learning and innovating, and in 1958 a new idea was brought to Cork. A group of leaders who had attended the centenary camp in

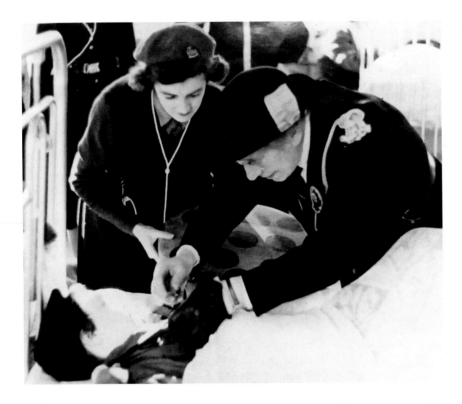

Miss K. Dale enrolling a Guide in the Orthopaedic Hospital in Cork.

Switzerland in 1957, had been impressed by the inclusion of people with disabilities (mostly children who had been injured during the war) at the camp, and decided to work with girls with disabilities in Cork. In early 1958, units were started in St Mary's Orthopaedic Hospital and the Spastic Clinic in Cork. The units were very successful, with outings being organised for the girls; they attended the 1961 Camp in Blarney, at which they had special accommodation. This ethos of inclusion was present from the beginning of Guiding and continues to be a core principle of the organisation. Since then the IGG has actively supported the inclusion of those with disabilities in Guiding through various initiatives including the Handicapped Committee and the Special Needs Committee. More recently, taking the example of the Equal Status Act 2000, the Irish Girl Guides prohibits discrimination on the grounds of marital status, family status, sexual orientation, religion, disability, race or membership of the Travelling community.

The Equality, Diversity and Inclusion Committee (EDI) of IGG was set up at a national level in order to promote and encourage special needs within Guiding and also to provide support to Leaders. There is also a Friend of the Disabled Badge that aims to provide girls with an insight into various disabilities. In every unit throughout the country there are children and leaders with a wide range of abilities and disabilities; each of them makes a unique contribution to their unit, and that contribution is equally valued and encouraged.

Lady Baden-Powell visited Ireland again in 1959. She was received by President Eamon de Valera and the first woman Lord Mayor of Cork, Jane Dowdall. At a rally held in her honour in the National Boxing Stadium in Dublin, there was a pageant of Irish handcrafts, songs and Irish dancing. Lady Baden-Powell was later honoured at City Hall and the Metropole Hotel in Cork. Her name tag simply read 'Herself', and it was as such that she was introduced to everyone. Although her five-day visit included a civic reception and numerous speeches, she always found time to stop and speak to the Guides and Brownies in the audience. She said:

> I care deeply and desperately about each Guide and each country. Each belongs to me. Guiding stems from the basic human desire to be, and to get, together, and so is indigenous to every country. I hope that my visit to Ireland will in some way help many more to share in the priceless programme for body, spirit and soul. From all the other Guides whom I represent, I bring you a message of goodwill, cheer, loving interest and challenge.

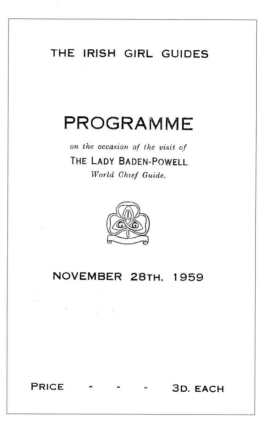

THE IRISH GIRL GUIDES

PROGRAMME

on the occasion of the visit of
THE LADY BADEN-POWELL
World Chief Guide.

NOVEMBER 28TH, 1959

PRICE   -   -   -   3D. EACH

Programme from the visit of Lady Baden-Powell in 1959.

CHAPTER 6

Guides and the Rising Tide

Ireland had suffered economically in the 1950s – jobs were scarce, and the economy was in a depressed state – but in 1959 Eamon de Valera became president and the new Taoiseach, Seán Lemass, began a programme to rebuild the economy. A key plank in this programme was to reconstruct the agricultural industry, and foreign companies were offered subsidies to cover up to two-thirds of the costs entailed in setting up factories in Ireland. The Irish economy grew rapidly, and exports increased by 50 percent between 1960 and 1966. The introduction of free secondary education in 1967 demonstrated that Ireland understood that access to education was fundamental to future social and economic prosperity.

Ireland also became more open in the 1960s and began to be influenced to a greater extent by American and European cultures. The 1960s and 1970s were also notable for the emergence of the women's-liberation movement, which successfully challenged some of the laws that discriminated against women and led to the formation of the Council for the Status of Women (later the National

An international group setting off on the Jubilee Trail in 1971.

Overleaf: *Dame Leslie Whately arriving for the opening of Leigh Dale Cottage in 1960.*

Women's Council). Ireland was prospering for the first time since the formation of the state in 1922.

The first major change for the Guides in this period was the building of the Irish Girl Guide Cottage in Cork. The project was to be a lasting memorial to Mrs Leigh-White, second director of the world bureau and area commissioner for County Cork, and Miss K. Dale, division commissioner in Cork. The cottage, called 'Leigh-Dale', was officially opened on 11 June 1960 by Dame Leslie Whateley, Director of the World Association of Girl Guides and Girl Scouts. In her speech, Leslie Whateley noted the contribution of the two women to Guiding and expressed her pride at having been asked to open the cottage:

> I have planted trees and laid foundation stones, but the world is so large that I have seldom been able to return to see those foundations grow into walls, nor the trees giving shade. In so many places Guides have surmounted seemingly insuperable difficulties to acquire a meeting place all their own. In every instance these dreams have come true through adult Guide leaders who have inspired and given help and encouragement to the girls to go on working to turn their dreams into reality. And so it is today, for we know it was Miss Dale's and Mrs Leigh-White's selfless work and love of Guiding and of young people which inspired you to possess and furnish this cottage as a lasting tribute to their memory.

Lady Baden-Powell at Leigh Dale Cottage in 1959.

Leigh Dale Cottage.

Other properties subsequently obtained by the IGG include Clonmel Cottage, in County Tipperary; Violet Hill, in County Clare; Glenaree and Glenstal, in County Limerick; Barnaribban, in County Sligo; the Guide Hall, in Ballina, County Mayo; Orchard Cottage, in County Cavan; The Demesne in Castlerea, County Roscommon; Mote Park, also in County Roscommon; Beech Cottage, in County Offaly; Kilkenny Scout and Guide Centre; Joint Scout and Guide Campsite, in Inistiogue, County Kilkenny; as well as premises in Cork, Galway and Limerick cities.

The term 'Senior Branch' was coined in 1960 to encompass all Ranger Companies, Sea Ranger Crews and Cadet Companies. This branch would cater for all those who had left Guides but were not ready to be adult leaders. Activities and trainings could now be organised under one heading – which made the administration of this age group much easier.

In 1961, celebrations were held countrywide to commemorate the Golden Jubilee of Guiding in Ireland, as well as the fiftieth anniversary of the founding of the first unit, in Harold's Cross, which was still active. According to the *Irish Times*:

> The voices of a thousand girls filled St Patrick's Cathedral, Dublin, yesterday, and the light blue

of a thousand uniforms provided a colourful contrast to the towering grey stone columns of the ancient building.

—⚬⚬⚬—

The Most Reverend Dr R. B. Pike, Bishop of Meath, commended the girls for the discipline, the order and the tidiness of all the companies present, and also reminded them of the importance of the Guide Promise and Law. As part of the Golden Jubilee, a concert took place on 16 March 1961 in the Olympia Theatre, Dublin. That summer, an international camp was held in Blarney, County Cork, in which girls from sixteen nations participated. Gill Buckley (neé McCullagh) of the Christ Church Guides, Dun Laoghaire recalls:

> In 1961, I seized the opportunity to go to the International Camp in Blarney. I was the only one from our Guides in 'Kenmare' sub-camp but I was just happy to be there. I loved the camp and really enjoyed meeting girls from Canada, the Netherlands,

A Sea Ranger practising her knots in the 1960s.

A view of Blarney Castle with camp in the foreground.

The gateway at the Blarney Camp. The letters were made of sods of turf.

Norway, etc. The camp was in the grounds of Blarney Castle. We could see the castle from our tent and when we went to 'kiss the Blarney Stone' we had an amazing view of the site. Our sub-camp and some others slept in bell tents, though some groups were using Icelandics. I don't remember how many Guides were there but looking at photos there were about fifty sleeping-tents.

The thing I remember most was going to fetch water. I enjoyed the camp so much I applied for and was selected as part of a group of fourteen who went to an International Camp in Denmark the following year. This was much larger – 14,000 girls. Lady Baden-Powell came to visit. She had something to say to everyone, just by looking at their uniform and badges. (I was helping with Brownies.) She said to me: 'Hello Pack Leader from Ireland.'

Jack Lynch, Minister for Industry and Commerce, visited the camp. Three hundred girls attended the event, where, according to the *Evening Echo*:

> The gay, fierce tarantella of Italy was danced . . . a mournful Maori song from New Zealand, accompanied by deftly handled sticks, was sung . . . a play of heaven, sad and joyful, was enacted by clear-spoken Swedes . . . and Norway's heritage of song further displayed another heritage, that of beautiful hand-embroidered costumes worn by the singers.

Trefoil News noted:

> One International Camp is so very different from another. That first campfire was an affair which made us proud to be Irish. Sitting round the circle we were entertained by performers whose acts were enhanced by the brilliance and beauty of their surroundings. The harpist in her magnificent red cloak sang so very sweetly that the valley seemed to echo for hours afterwards with the melody of the Irish tunes, and the feet of the Irish dancers held our eyes as if they were

Leaders gathered around the gypsy caravan in Blarney.

strong magnets. I only hope the Guides from overseas enjoyed that evening as much as the Irish Guides did, or did they prefer the following Saturday when they performed in their national costumes in front of a large Irish crowd of visitors?

⸻⟋⟍⟍⸻

The first time the Irish Girl Guides hosted a large-scale international conference was in 1964, when a World Association Course for trainers was held at An Grianán, Termonfeckin, County Louth. The organisation was galvanised by the size of the task ahead of them, and everyone, 'both in uniform and out', helped with the plans. There were representatives – top-level trainers – from twenty-eight countries; judging by the letters received from them after their departure, the course was a great success, and their appreciation of the hospitality they received was very sincere. Elspeth Henderson (who went on to become the President of the Irish Girl Guides 2002-2005) remembers:

> I was a Sea Ranger at the time and was responsible for looking after the needs of delegates. It was my first experience of

Previous: *A sing-song at the 1961 Blarney Camp.*

an international event for leaders, and I remember being so impressed by those who attended. It was amazing to me to see how people communicated, regardless of their language.

━━◦◦◦◦━━

A concerted effort was made for members to be seen in the St Patrick's Day Parades in the 1960s: groups took part in the Dublin, Cork and Limerick celebrations. In 1965, the Guides could be seen cooking sausages on the float as they travelled down O'Connell Street: the float was 'highly recommended' in the competition for best float.

A Thinking Day Pageant was held in the Concert Hall of the RDS in Dublin in 1969. A special train was put on from Cork, and the platform in Kent Station was a sight to behold. At Connolly Station in Dublin, girls piled off the train and onto double-decker buses, which brought them to Ballsbridge. There were various scenes and nations represented during the ceremony. Even the 'World' was in attendance. He was seen as a stooped figure to begin with, but then, as he realised the work that Guides worldwide were doing for him, his condition improved markedly. There were various comments made about the quality of the pageant. A Ranger Guider from Great Britain said:

I am so glad I stayed on in Dublin and saw the pageant. It was magnificent and I would not have missed it for anything.

━━◦◦◦◦━━

A teacher remembers:

I was thrilled. I had no idea the Irish Girl Guides had such worldwide contacts and joined in so many activities everywhere.

Irish delegates at the 20th World Conference in Finland in 1969.

A major change to the uniform of the association was made in the 1960s, when the Brownie uniform was changed from brown to blue. The Girl Guides uniform is something that is very particular to them and marks them out as different from other youth organisations. For that reason, it is essential that girls are proud to wear it, and that it is comfortable and modern. So, as times change, so does the uniform. Eileen Beatty, writing in *Trefoil News* in 1957, remembers what her uniform meant to her when she began her career in the Guides:

> Sometimes when I see Guides buying uniforms at HQ it seems rather matter of fact, but I do believe that for most of them the excitement is just the same as we experienced when we bought our first uniforms of scratchy navy blue serge blouse and skirt, the wide-brimmed hat with chin strap worn very dashingly on the point of the chin, the white haversack, belt, tie, etc. Do the Guides of today realise how lucky they are not having a white haversack? It was worn on the back like a school satchel, with the bands coming over the shoulders and under the arms. To make it really smart, it had to be starched so stiffly that one's arms were practically cut off at the shoulder. And the horrible button on the haversack that invariably got entangled in the plaited hair. Getting uniform ready in those days took time, with the starched haversack and tie, and the hat whose brim had to be pressed over a damp cloth to take the waves of it off.
>
> But our Guiders were really smart. Full uniform was a navy coat and skirt, and white shirt with pale blue tie. Lieutenant had three chevrons on the left arm to denote her rank, but Captain had the

distinction of wearing cock's feathers, where her hat was turned up at the side, and of course carried a walking stick! Very smart, but times have changed – and, we hope, for the better. Now we are busily engaged in deciding on a pattern for shorts for Guides to be worn in camp. How many inches above the knee? Well! Well!

———◦◦◦———

Over the years, the uniform of each branch underwent many revamps, modernisations and changes, but it always maintained at its core its smartness, practicality and ease of care. When a Guide walks down the street in uniform, people should know immediately that she is a Guide. Sometimes, however, the uniform gave girls cause to laugh, as Hazel Murphy from Eastern Region recalls:

Putting up a washing line at camp in 1973.

I remember one weekend camping when our local commissioner called to say 'hello' and examine us in some badges. Where we had to sit on groundsheets for our meals, she got to sit on an upturned biscuit tin. Then we all got a good view of her navy bloomers. These bloomers were an invaluable part of the Guide uniform. If they were large enough, they could come up as far as your bra and down as far as the tops of your knees. A very useful item of clothing, as it could also be used for putting up flagpoles.

Guides removing ivy from trees in the 1970s.

In 1970, when commemorating sixty years of Guiding, Lady Baden-Powell wrote:

> We've done it! In these 'sixty years of distance run', large numbers of great people have thought and striven and planned with care, and pushed and pulled and worked with a will to build up Guiding for thousands and thousands to enjoy and benefit from. With justifiable pride and delight, we can rejoice over the achievements of the past, and with stout-hearted confidence look forward to the same successful progress in the future. May this Diamond Jubilee Year refresh our energies and bring joyous renewed enthusiasm to one and all.

Nineteen seventy was declared European Conservation Year: members of the IGG attended a weekend in Avondale for Guides. They joined in the coastal dead-bird counts, planted trees and berried bushes, cut ivy from trees, joined in anti-litter campaigns and organised competitions. Those who participated in these activities were awarded the new Conservation badge.

In 1970, for the first time, the Irish Girl Guides received financial assistance from the government, with the Department of Education awarding the organisation a grant of £1,000 'for training and publications'. This connection with the Department of Education and the support of government funding continues to the present day. As a result of this new income, and the massive growth of the organisation (in 1969 there were 5,334 members and by 1975 this had increased to 10,324 and by 1978 it had reached 16,022), it was decided that a regular staff should be employed. (Up to this point, all posts had been manned by volunteers.) It was also decided to invest in up-to-date office equipment to enable the IGG to be run more efficiently.

Celebrations of the sixtieth anniversary of Guiding in Ireland began in February with a reception at Headquarters at 16 St Stephen's Green, Dublin. The Taoiseach's wife, Mrs Maureen Lynch, was presented with a set of Guide gifts in Celtic design, which had been specially designed for the Jubilee year.

In May, a rally for Guides from all over Ireland was held at Lansdowne Road. In July, Guides held a major national camp, with three hundred Guides in attendance, on the

Guides rafting.

military camp at the Curragh, County Kildare. According to the *Evening Herald*:

> Three hundred pints of milk a day, eighty-six loaves of bread, twenty-three dozen eggs. Food enough to feed an army, one might say. The army in question is a group of schoolgirls from the Irish Girl Guides.
>
> A coach carrying forty-four international visitors from eight countries travelled around Ireland on a 'Jubilee Trail', visiting the camp en route. In August, an international camp for Rangers and Senior Guides was held at Kilruddery in County Wicklow.

A shopping expedition in the Distribution Centre.

In 1971, a member of the IGG hit the headlines when she used her first-aid, swimming and life-saving skills to save the lives of three young men. Fifteen-year-old Michelle Duffin, a member of Greystones Girl Guide Company, was credited with saving the lives of the men, at the North Beach at Greystones, on 5 June 1971. The account stated that four men went out in a small boat and the boat capsized. Local fishermen said it was too rough to go out to the men. A speedboat from the harbour was able to rescue one of them, but the other three were left floundering. Michelle took a rope which was about to be thrown towards the drowning men and, according to an account given by Vivienne Flynn and published in the *Wicklow People* on 19 June 1971:

> swam out to the boat and tied the rope to it, and held two of the men who couldn't swim at all. She then told the men on the beach to pull the boat in by the rope, which they did, pulling boat, men and Michelle safely to shore.

Overleaf: Guides marching in the St Patrick's Day Parade in Clonmel in 1979.

In the same year, a new Guide shop, to sell merchandise and uniforms to members, was officially opened in Cork. The opening ceremony was attended by the Lord Mayor. This was the first shop of its kind to be opened outside Dublin.

Also in 1971, a new flag for the IGG was introduced. The existing flag, which featured the cross of St Patrick, was replaced with one which simply featured the Guide Trefoil on a green background, with the motto 'Be Prepared' underneath.

President Childers at the official launch of the regionalisation scheme in 1973.

A major restructuring of the Irish Girl Guides began in 1973. Due to the growth in numbers, and to aid organisation, the administration of the association was divided into seven regions, with the aim of achieving 'regionalisation not isolation'. There would be a regional commissioner who would work in consultation with a Regional Secretary. The regions were to be self-sustaining financially, but for the first year each region would be given a float. The new regions were North-West, West and Central Midlands, Mid-West, South-West, South-East, Eastern, and North-East. The work of the region would be administered by regional meetings, and a representative from this meeting would report back to the executive committee. Each region was to elect their own representatives to various national committees, and was also to organise trainings and 'fun days'. This scheme was piloted for two years, and soon afterwards the geographical split of the new regions was adjusted, but on the whole the scheme worked well – and remains the basis of the administration of the Irish Girl Guides.

Regionalisation proved to be a big success, and allowed local members to focus on Guiding within specific boundaries. Guiding flourished in the newly formed regions; one example of this was in the newly formed Mid-West Region, which covered counties Limerick, Clare and Tipperary. Guiding was practically non-existent in the region before the 1970s, although there had been a Guide Company in Cashel in the mid-fifties, and in the early seventies there were a couple of units in Limerick city and one in Nenagh. After the new region had been formed, Pat Snow, the regional commissioner, was told to 'get Guiding going down there'. The challenge was accepted, and Pat, with some committed Guiders, set to work; within a short space of time, units had sprung up all over the region.

With the growth of the region, it was decided that outdoor centres were needed to maintain the numbers and allow leaders to learn the skills necessary to camp with their girls. Violet Hill in Clare, Glenaree in Limerick, and Belgian Cottage in Glenstal Abbey were procured through dedicated fund-raising, which ranged from 'knitting squares for blankets in the window of a Limerick store' to Christmas carolling. In 1990, following the sale of Glenaree, a new premises was bought in Edward Street, Limerick, to house a regional headquarters and distribution centre. Irene Reale (from Thurles) attributes the success of the region to the fact that the 'development of the leader as well as the girls has always been important in Mid-West, so we work in teams where possible, to support and encourage members to progress towards indoor and outdoor qualifications'.

There had been many changes in the organisation, uniform and programme of the Irish Girl Guides during the late 1960s and early 1970s. The Guides' longevity is witnessed by the movement's ability to evolve and adapt to the social and economic circumstances of the country. Rapid changes were taking place in Ireland. The economy had improved during the 1960s under the leadership of Seán Lemass, and in 1973, along with the United Kingdom, Ireland joined the European Economic Community. On joining the EEC, the government had to abandon the marriage bar - under which women working in the public service had to leave their jobs when they got married - and introduce equal pay. Women were now, legally, equal to men. Guiding in Ireland was entering a new world – one in which they would have the same opportunities as their male counterparts.

CHAPTER 7

The New Ireland

If the sixties had seen changes, the seventies would witness even more, both in Ireland and in Guiding. The Irish Girl Guides had to leave 16 St Stephen's Green as the property was being sold. However, the owners provided new premises at 27 Pembroke Park in Donnybrook. In 1973, the first nationwide fund-raiser for the Headquarters Capital Fund was held. In no time at all, the fund was ready to be used, and work began on converting the new building. The IGG named the building 'Trefoil House', and it was officially opened by the then director of the world bureau, Lyn Joynt. Trefoil House is still the administrative centre of the IGG. The building houses a room named after the Powerscourts, and in 1994 an extension was added, which includes a room named after former chief commissioner and president Eileen Beatty. A letter which appeared in the *Irish Press* in November 1974 praised the Girl Guides on the refurbishment of the premises in Pembroke Park:

A Guide and Scout marry in 1977.

Trefoil House.

Next-door neighbours are apt to be very important to each other, either as friends or nuisance. We find our next-door neighbours, the Irish Girl Guides Organisation, grand friendly, helpful people.

Pembroke Park is ageing now, and they have refurbished the lovely old house. They will keep up appearances.

The Guides' work of encouraging order in youth when youth is tempted to disorder is gravely important. Parents need their help in this most freedom-loving age, when youth demands the maximum of liberty and needs Guidance in using it.

The Guides are the biggest Jewish youth club. Of the majority, 60 percent are Catholic and the rest Protestants. Their literature reveals their character – forming methods. They encourage the Irish language. Their influence over a period will be found excellent in any district.

Bryan W. Roche 25 Pembroke Park

In 1974, Kitty Richardson was appointed Secretary General of the Irish Girl Guides, based in Trefoil House. She had responsibility for the administration and day-to-day running of the IGG. She would hold the post for twenty-two years, during which time, as *Trefoil News* reported in December 1997, she always:

> Found time to listen, advise, and share the fun with everyone from the newest Brownie to the chief commissioner.

A long tradition was started by Rangers in 1977 when they took part in the first Ventact (or 'Venture Activities', named for the Venture Scouts, the scouting counterparts of Rangers) camp, which was held in Larch Hill, County Dublin. Ventact, which is organised by a joint committee of Scouting and Guiding, caters for Venture Scouts and Ranger Guides from all over Ireland. The event takes place during the first weekend in September each year at the Killcully Scout Centre in Cork. It is one of the highlights of the year for every Venturer and Ranger.

In the 1970s, with dramatic changes in camping practices, it was becoming easier for Guides to go camping on a whim. Large, bulky frame tents and bell tents were being replaced by new, lighter tents with stainless-steel and aluminium poles, and flysheets made of nylon and polyester. All of these developments made the tents stronger and more portable than before, and hiking with everything in a rucksack was now a much easier task than it had been in the past. This facilitated an increase in camping activities. Lorna Finnegan from Drogheda recalls:

Guides at camp in Tarbert in 1982.

> Camping: even today, the word evokes happy, magical memories for me. Cooking on patrol fires, building bridges, sleeping under the stars, hiking to the lake . . . . My love of the outdoors was well and truly born. While the memories of the activities have faded as the years have passed, what hasn't faded are the memories of the women who

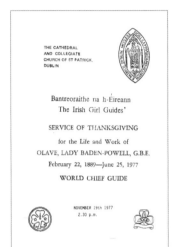

The programme for the service of Thanksgiving held for Olave Baden-Powell in St Patrick's Cathedral Dublin.

Opposite: *Howth Brownies, 1984.*

challenged us to explore, and shared their love of the outdoors with us. Your spirit lives on in the lives of those you touched. Thank you.

〰️

The world of Guiding was rocked in June 1977 by the announcement of the death of Lady Baden-Powell, World Chief Guide. Like her husband, she had prepared a last message for her 'family' in November 1973:

Dear Guides, Scouts, Cubs and Brownies and all their leaders and friends:

I shall have left this world when you receive this message, which I leave to express my thanks for all the kindnesses and the affection shown to me, and to say how greatly I rejoiced over the way in which you have all carried out your share in the work of the movement that my beloved husband invented for the advancement of boys and girls of all countries, years ago.

*Brownies form a
Guard of Honour
for the wedding of
their leader.*

I have firm belief in Almighty God and in the life in the world to
come, when he and I will be reunited, and together we shall watch
over you who have been enrolled as members of this world family, and
go on caring for your progress and your well-being.

I trust that you will continue fully to use the system of work and play
that our movement provides, keeping up the fun and friendships made
at your meetings and camps, abiding by the Promise and upholding
the Laws that you undertook to live by when you joined up.

In that way you will not only advance yourself in body, mind and
spirit, but you will affect those around you, in doing what is honourable
and right and wise, and in giving out kindness of thought and action,
thus striving against all ills and helping to make the world a happier
and better place in which to live.

I trust you will be successful in all your tasks, and may God be with
you in the coming years.

Opposite: *Brownies
in Dundrum
dancing round a
toadstool in 1975.*

After a private cremation service, the World Chief Guide's ashes were flown to
Kenya to be buried with her husband's remains in his grave at Nyeri. Kenya
declared the Baden-Powell's' grave a national monument in 2001. Thanksgiving
services were held in Westminster Abbey and St Patrick's Cathedral, which was
full to capacity.

In September 1979, Pope John Paul II visited Ireland, for the first and only
time. On a beautiful September day, he said Mass to more than a million people
in the Phoenix Park; the crowds included a large contingent from the Irish Girl

Guides. They set off early in the morning: even those who lived in Dublin had to get up at 5 AM to get a spot where they could hold their flag high for the day.

One Guider remembers the panic she experienced when she lost a Guide: it transpired that the girl was safe at home in her bed. The memories of the day live on in the hearts of the girls who attended. The response to the Pope's visit was unprecedented, and provoked a religious fervour previously unseen on the streets of Ireland. His now-famous words 'Young people of Ireland, I love you' resonated with people, particularly those involved in youth organisations, and touched both Catholics and non-Catholics in Ireland. One Guide, Fióna Walsh from Dundrum, remembers:

> It was an amazing experience to be in uniform with all our friends, and for some reason it didn't matter what religion you were. We were right beside the altar and the Pope mobile swept right by us. It was a long but very memorable day.

The seventieth anniversary of the IGG, on 2 May 1981, presented the association with a huge opportunity to raise its public profile. A Festival of Guiding was organised in Cork; it was opened by the president of Ireland, Patrick Hillery. (As it was also the president's birthday, the Guides sang 'Happy Birthday' to him.) The festival was the first national 'fun day' which had been organised for many years; the estimated attendance was ten thousand. The event was held in Páirc Uí Chaoimh, which was provided free by the GAA. There was no entry fee, but all attendees were encouraged to donate money to the Irish Kidney Association for the purchase of a portable dialysis unit. Donations amounted to £4,000; the money, which came in all denominations (including £100 in 1p coins), took seven hours to count. Violet Warner, the organiser of the event, remembers the day being hectic, as a number of political events converged to make things difficult for the president. As he sat on the rostrum enjoying the events Violet spent the afternoon giving him updates on an Aer Lingus flight which had been hijacked. There were also protests in the locality, as Bobby Sands was approaching the end of his hunger strike. However, those present knew nothing of the excitement outside the stadium and were simply enjoying the day. Logistically, it was a massive event: many of those who had travelled long distances stayed overnight in Páirc Uí Chaoimh and local schools; others came for the day and brought picnics with them. 'E.M.T.' a member of Trefoil Guild, wrote in *Trefoil News* in 1981:

Festival of Guiding, in Cork, with President Hillery addressing the participants.

> Our impression of the festival was one of admiration [for] the amazing work that went into the smooth running of such a large gathering, the care and attention given to all the thousands of Brownies and Guides. Cork has every right to be proud of its commissioners and Guiders for seeing the programme through.

As part of the celebrations, 56,000 daffodil bulbs were planted all over Ireland. (Many of them are still blooming, including those at Leigh-Dale Cottage in Cork.) The official end of the Jubilee year was celebrated at a concert in the RDS. Guides who had travelled from around the country were given accommodation

JUBILEE CONCERT

PROGRAMME

THE IRISH GIRL GUIDES

1911-1981

R.D.S.

31st October 1981

The Jubilee celebrations culminated with a concert in the RDS, October 1981.

by their sister Guides in the city; for many, it was their first experience of the national and international nature of Guiding, and many new friendships were forged throughout the Jubilee year. During the Jubilee year, almost £200,000 was raised, and the IKA was presented with the dialysis machine.

Integration and inclusion are central tenets of the Guiding ethos, and in the summer of 1981 the first Camp Curlew was held. This camp was specifically designed for children who could not attend camp due to physical disabilities. The camp was held in Santa Sabina School, Sutton, County Dublin. Patrol leaders and adult leaders from surrounding units came to help and participate in the camp, and the girls slept on mattresses in the school hall. Just like at any other camp, the girls swam, had campfires and went on outings. After the first Camp Curlew, other similar camps, both indoors and outdoors, were held. There were camps for girls with learning difficulties, from the Travelling community and from disadvantaged areas. The National Memorial Cottage in Enniskerry was made accessible to those with physical disabilities. These camps highlighted the inclusive nature of Guiding: girls of all abilities and from all backgrounds could join and feel that they belonged, and they learnt to be tolerant and accepting of those who were different from them.

Nineteen eighty-two saw Guides contribute to the move of the World Association to new premises in London. The funds for the move were to be raised by means of a request for every member to contribute the equivalent of £1 sterling. However, since this would place a very heavy burden on members from poorer countries, the IGG

Four Guides celebrate Thinking Day in Cork, 1981.

decided that each member would be asked to contribute £1.25 to alleviate the pressure for their less well-off sisters, and the amount was raised relatively quickly. Due to collections held by all national organisations and friends of Girl Guiding and Girl Scouting, the World Bureau was able to move to its new premises in 1984. The money collected in Ireland was used to purchase carpets made in County Cork for the new offices. That year also saw laminated identity cards being issued to all warranted leaders for the first time.

Brownies playing dress-up.

Listening to the young people involved in the organisation has always been central to its success, and in 1982 the Young Advisers Council was established by the then chief commissioner, Audrey Carr. The council provided a channel of communication for the ideas of Guiders in the eighteen-to-thirty age group to the executive committee and other national committees; it was also given the responsibility of sending two members to the National Youth Council of Ireland. It was deemed to be important that young Guiders be involved in a real way with all aspects of the IGG and to inform themselves of developments within the organisation. They were also to explore any items that were of particular relevance to the under-thirties. The council members began organising and participating in various events within the organisation. One of the most successful of these events was a weekend in Enniskerry with the Ulster Junior Council; this was followed by a return visit to Lorne, near Belfast. These marked the beginning of various twinning events. The council also organised seminars in effective communication, produced special editions of *Trefoil News*, ran a National Guiders Forum for Guiders in the

eighteen-to-thirty age group, and ran a National Youth Forum for Patrol Leaders, Rangers and Young Leaders. The Council noted in its report that:

> Ireland is a country with a young population. The IGG has to show that it is interested and aware of what is going on and prepared to get involved with the problems of today. We have the ability, the youth, the leadership; let's look to the future!

Opposite: Members taking part in Youth Week, Athlone 1986.

As part of these new initiatives, a new tier was added to the leadership system, with the introduction of the category of Young Leaders (girls who were too old to be Guides but too young to be leaders), under the auspices of the National Training Committee.

Being responsible leaders has never stopped Senior Branch from having adventures, and in 1984 three Rangers from Cork became the first IGG team to participate in the Explorer Belt in Sweden. In the Explorer Belt, teams are sent to an unknown destination in another country. They carry all their equipment for ten days, find their own campsites and navigate their way over 200 km to a predetermined end point. The event had been run by and for Scouts for many years. Rose Hennessy from Midleton, who was a member of the 1984 team, remembers:

Sense of adventure.

> Waking up next to this mirror-like, still lake, with a mist hanging over it and surrounded by forest, and feeling so adventurous and independent with my team of three. Taking part in the expedition was one of the markers in my life that I know shaped me into the person I am.

The Scouts would continue to invite the IGG to join with them in this expedition every two years; on occasion, the IGG even helped organise it. In 2006, however, following the amalgamation of the two Scout associations, they simply could no longer accommodate the numbers that were interested and the Guides had to stop taking part in the Scout-organised event. Lisa (Finan) McSweeney, from the UK, recalls:

Adult leaders tackle the Explorer Belt in Spain.

> For me, the Explorer Belt was one of the greatest personal challenges I'd ever taken on. It proved to be just that, an amazing challenge, a wonderful experience, and one of my greatest life-defining events. One of the best things about being involved with the IGG is that we are consistently given opportunities to develop and grow as individuals, and there is always a challenge to complete and a goal to strive for. For me, walking the incredible distance was just part of it. My partner and I fully embraced the Spanish culture and met some amazing people along the way. We saw some wonderful sights, burst each other's blisters, laughed with each other and cried with each other. We hugged tightly and enjoyed the euphoria when we were awarded our Explorer Belts! Of course there was another amazing thing to come out of that Explorer Belt . . . it is where I met my husband. We've been together ever since and have 3 future Explorer Belters on our hands.

Following this successful foray in 1982, a similar event was held in Connemara in 1985. This was the forerunner of what was to become the Chief Commissioner's Award – with the first award being made in Dingle in 1993. This event is now held every two years: the task is a survival challenge for the participants, who, as part of teams of two or three members, complete a hiking expedition of 60 km over five days, undertaking a number of projects en route. The venue for the event is a well-guarded secret: participants don't know what part of Ireland they will be hiking in until they arrive the night before the event. Rose Hennessy from Midleton, who was one of the organisers of the event, remembers:

> This was the second Chief Commissioner's Award run by the IGG and the first time that the structure mirrored the Explorer Belt. I remember the sense of achievement and pride in setting off the teams and welcoming them back in at the end. I remember the award ceremony at Gallarus Oratory, and we were cloaked in a Kerry mist that for me was atmospheric . . . for others maybe just wet! I felt I had come full circle.

*Participating in the Chief
Commissioner's Award is a
demanding challenge.*

Over the years, hundreds of women (young and old, fit and unfit) have taken part in the Explorer Belt and Chief Commissioner's Award. Participants always look back on these events fondly and with pride.

Nineteen eighty-five was a busy year for Guides, since it was both International Youth Year (IYY) and the seventy-fifth anniversary of the founding of Girl Guides internationally. The twenty-fifth world conference of WAGGGS was held in New York in 1984. The IGG sent two delegates and two visitors, who voted on a variety of issues 'related to the girl and how it would affect the Brownies, Guides and Rangers etc'. The theme of the conference was 'International Youth Year – participation, development and peace'.

The establishment of a joint Guide/Scout IYY committee marked the first occasion when the four Guide and Scout associations jointly organised a common national programme for the Guides and Scouts of Ireland. Their programme included a Youth Forum for older Guides and Rangers. One of the topics the forum discussed was the issue of Guides being a single-sex organisation; in 1985, it was decided to maintain the status quo.

After marking the international beginning of Guiding in 1985, the IGG celebrated their own seventy-fifth anniversary in 1986. One of the main events was 'a thanksgiving and celebration for seventy-five years of Guiding, held in the National Concert Hall in Dublin on 11 October 1986, with a cast of 450'. The programme was 'designed to illustrate the various facets of Guiding: the Promise and Law; camping; campfire; friendship; international aspects; conservation; fun; service; and history of Guiding', Joy Clarke of Blackrock recalls. The president of Ireland, Patrick Hillery, wrote a message in the visitors' book, wishing the Guides 'congratulations and best wishes' and saying 'long may the Irish Girl Guides continue its successful work in the promotion of self-development and self-reliance'.

As part of the celebrations, a national camp was held at Ballyfin College, County Laois, with Guides, Rangers and Young Leaders from the seven regions, and international guests from as far afield as Japan and New Zealand. On the Sunday morning, RTÉ broadcast the ecumenical service from the camp. The camp ended on Saturday 23 August. Hurricane 'Charlie' arrived on Monday morning, just before the large marquees were taken down! Mary Shepherd of Eastern Region remembers:

Camp booklet from Siamsa Ballyfin, 1986.

> Friday's closing campfire by New Zealand's popular Guider Penny Lamsdale was rousing. At the end, Camp Chief Kitty [Richardson] was given a standing ovation as all the campers present showed their appreciation of a camp to be proud of, united, uplifted, blessed both in weather and in spirit – a perfect celebration of seventy-five years of Guiding.

For the first time since the introduction of Rangers in 1918, a new branch was started in 1985. This had been inspired by a commissioner's conference which had been held in Ulster in October of that year. The IGG's representatives, Hazel Newman and Joy Clarke, brought the idea to the executive committee as it was thought that it would be good for the association to encourage younger girls, under seven years old, to join. On 6 December 1985, the executive committee gave permission to start a pilot programme for five- to seven-and-a-half-year-old

girls in a unit in Ballybrack, Dublin. The Ballybrack unit was started on 22 February 1986 – Thinking Day. It was decided to call Ladybird leaders 'Coccinella' (the well-known black-and-red ladybird). Heather Kuss, who was asked to be involved in the pilot unit in Ballybrack, reported that:

> The group has been running for just over one year and consists of twelve five- to seven-year-olds. This age group integrates very well. . . . Lively and familiar games are enjoyed by all, as are skipping, ball games and craft work. Team games are popular also, but discussions are less so, as this group seems to prefer activity (particularly the younger ones).

Opposite: *Ladybird Guides join the association.*

After narrowing the choice of names for the new branch down to twelve, the final decision was to call it 'Ladybirds'. They would have a uniform of a navy tracksuit with red Ladybird motif, red neckerchief, navy socks, dark runners and a pale blue T-shirt. By 1988, the Irish Girl Guides could report that 'Ladybirds . . . has proved popular and additional units have been started'. In September 1989, the Ladybirds were officially launched by Minister for Education Mary O'Rourke. By the time of the 1989 annual report there were thirty-three Ladybird units operating in six of the seven regions countrywide. The age bands for members had been changed; the youngest member could now be as young

Overleaf: *Rangers and Sea Rangers at the presentation of the 1st Ranger Challenge in 1986.*

as five years of age, with no upper age limit. Karina Dingerkus, of North-West Region, recalls:

> I remember one of the first Ladybird units that was set up after I started. The girls arrived and they were all very shy, hiding among and clinging onto their mums' legs. Within three weeks the little girls were running into the community centre, all chat and ready to go. It was a real inspiration to see how quickly they settled into Guiding.

The Ranger Challenge was introduced in 1986. The format included seven challenges on different topics, which included international, entertainment, hiking and community service. The Ross Cup, which had been in use since the start of Guiding in Ireland, was to be presented to the winners of the Community Service challenge. There was also a Ranger Cup, which would be presented for overall success. The Ranger Challenge subsequently became the Senior Branch Challenge, which is now run every second year and can be completed by groups of Senior Branchers or individuals.

Irish Guiding continued to flourish internationally and produce people who would go on to work at high levels in the various organisations. It was with great pride that in 1989 Ireland celebrated the election of one of its own, Elspeth

The winners of the first Ranger Challenge: Sirius Sea Rangers from Cork.

Henderson, as chairman of the WAGGGS Europe Region Committee (she remained in this position until 1995).

It is often stated that large-scale job losses and recession means more volunteers. However, the 1988 annual report made an interesting comment on the economic circumstances of the time, stating that 'it would seem that unemployment has a greater impact on leaders in an all-female organisation who being firstly, in many cases, housewives, and in their spare time youth leaders, find themselves needed even more in their homes if their husbands do not have a job'. There were not enough women available to become leaders in the late 1980s and as a result existing leaders were stretched to capacity. The existing members (many of whom would normally have become leaders on turning eighteen) had no jobs and no opportunities in Ireland and were forced to emigrate. Finding leaders became harder and harder for the Irish Girl Guides. As Robert Baden-Powell once said: 'Leadership is the keynote to success – but leadership is difficult to define, and leaders are difficult to find.' However, although leaders were hard to find, it seems that girls were not, and in the 1980s membership was at its peak, hitting a high of more than 20,000 members countrywide. Guiding was expanding rapidly, and was now in parts of the country it had never been in before, particularly in Munster and Connacht. Massive work was being done nationally to spread Guiding and girls and adults who had never previously considered joining the movement were embracing it. As Fióna Walsh of Dundrum notes:

> The best thing about Guiding is the warm and fuzzy feeling we all get from being with like-minded people, and the wonderful friendships which we have formed thanks to Guiding!

President Mary Robinson at the unveiling of the Lives Lost at Sea Mounument, Howth 1994.

The 1990s began with the election as president of Mary Robinson, a feminist politician and lawyer, ending seventy years of male domination of Ireland's presidency. Her visibility and vibrancy had a huge impact on Ireland's international status and on the way in which Irish women saw themselves. For years, the IGG had tried to instil in its members the belief that they could achieve their potential; now Ireland was beginning to change to reflect that belief.

CHAPTER 8

Ireland and the Celtic Tiger

W ork and pay conditions in Ireland for women had been improving continually since the country joined the EEC. The Celtic Tiger of the 1990s and 2000s can in part be attributed to 'a marked increase of 400,000 or 60 percent in the number of women at work in Ireland since the mid-1990s. . . . The introduction of a national minimum wage, enhanced child-care services, increased maternity leave and increased child benefit have enabled women to meet both their work and family commitments'[†]. It may have been as a result of this increase in women entering the workplace that volunteering was affected in a negative way and membership numbers began to fall. In 1990, membership was 17,179; by 1991, it had fallen to 15,616.

The problem was not just in Ireland, however: the early 1990s was a time of uncertainty across Guiding in Europe: membership dropped in all member countries, and as a result WAGGGS launched a recruitment campaign and encouraged all national organisations to do the same. Ireland, which was struggling not just to increase membership but to maintain the numbers that

Camp at Mount Mellary, 1991. (Courtesy of the Irish Examiner)

[†] John Maloney, TD, March 2010 in a statement to the Commission on the Status of Women.

Three Chief Commissioners in 1976: Frances Dwyer, Eileen Beatty and Marjorie Williams.

were there, was set the challenge of increasing membership by 5 percent over three years. In the annual report of 1990, it was noted that 'in order to maintain our numbers, let alone increase them, we must have sufficient trained leaders. Unemployment, emigration and the increase in the number of working mothers are some of the factors making it more difficult to attract leaders'. Nonetheless, this did not undermine the commitment of the leaders who were still involved: it was noted in the 1990 annual review that 'we are fortunate in the Irish Girl Guides in having many dedicated leaders, of all ages, highly trained and with a wide variety of skills'. The leaders in the IGG have more often than not occupied a special place in the hearts of their charges. They are inspirational, selfless and hard-working women who, whether they give a year or ninety years to the organisation, make an indelible mark on the girls they work with. Ollie Ballantine, who has been both a child and adult member, put it well:

Alison Hirschberg, Assistant Chief, planting a tree at North East Regional Conference during the 1980s.

> When I say 'Guiding', what I really mean are those incredible women who I encountered throughout my years from shy and uncertain Guide to idealistic Ranger, to a woman who is still inspired by their vision, their enthusiasm and their belief in the possibility that we can still change the world. We called them the 'big mommas' and we were endlessly amazed by their faith in us and their endless energy and encouragement of our often madcap schemes. They saw absolutely nothing out of the ordinary when we suggested building pioneering structures in Dublin city centre to raise money for children in need. They found the funds to get us qualified in Mountain Leadership, supported our schemes to get Senior Branch Guides and Scouts away on mountain weekends, and had the imagination to dream up so many initiatives so that as many girls as possible would get a chance to experience the adventure and excitement of being part of this worldwide movement.
>
> As I stood in the middle of a food distribution to malnourished children and their families in Angola, it was my experience of people management that I'd learnt in Guides that gave me the confidence

Emer O'Sullivan, Chief Commissioner, and Dilys Lindsay, President.

and creativity to organise the chaos into some sort of order, and it was the feedback and encouragement from 'big mommas' that often re-energised me when I felt less than able to do this work.

What impresses me most about the women I've been lucky enough to know through Guiding is that each one of them remains young, with a thirst to learn more, to be better, and with a conviction that it's still worth trying to change the world.

Members of Executive, and Programme and Training

It was decided in 1990 to streamline the organisation of the IGG in order to allow for more efficient management of its members. The size of the executive committee was reduced, with the representatives of the main branches and committees linked together in a new committee, the Development Committee (which continues today as 'Programme and Training'), with overall responsibility for the coordination and development of the programme of each branch and ensuring that all leaders are trained for their roles within the association, leaving the executive committee to deal with administration and policy. It was also decided to bring the Rangers and Young Leaders together under one name, Senior Branch (although this term was in use since the 1960s, it was only properly embraced in the 1990s). In the same year, a new *Handbook for Guiders* was launched. This book, which is constantly updated, would go on to become the Bible for all leaders within the organisation.

The suffering that followed the meltdown of the nuclear reactor in Chernobyl in 1986 affected the Irish people deeply. All over the country, people gave aid in any way they could. As part of this national outpouring of grief, in the summer of 1990 the four Irish Guide and Scout associations offered hospitality to a party of forty children from Chernobyl for a month. The IGG hosted eleven girls and one adult, together with an Irish interpreter, at camps in Mount Nugent and Glenaree, and organised home hospitality in Drogheda and Dublin, and a week-long holiday in Violet Hill cottage in Broadford. Mary Clarke of Howth remembers:

First camp held with the children from Chernobyl 1990.

> The first group literally had what they stood up in and one change of clothes. We guessed that someone had dressed them in the airport before they left, as they obviously came from very bad circumstances.

The link was repeated in 1991: the children from Chernobyl attended a camp in Mount Mellary, County Waterford, then stayed with local families and participated in activities during the day. The visits were challenging in terms of the language barrier, culture and food, but all involved also found them rewarding, fun and laughter-filled. During both visits, the children were welcomed with open arms not just by the Guides and Scouts but also by the local communities. Businesses were incredibly generous, and people opened their homes to the visitors. Many people who met the children in the 1990s have maintained contact with them and have organised independent visits since then.

Guides also signed up to Concern's Trees for Africa appeal to 'buy trees and to plant in cooperation with the Irish relief agency Concern in Tanzania [and to] create awareness amongst our members about environmental problems in Third World countries'. The money was raised by individual units, who devised their own fund-raising schemes, with the final fund-raising taking place at the National Camp in Mount Melleray. Concern was presented with a cheque for £10,000, which provided for the planting of fifty thousand trees.

The social-mindedness of Guides was both national and international: in 1991, in conjunction with the Irish Wheelchair Association, more than £60,000 was raised through a national strategy of bag-packing and other fund-raising efforts for the Fast Forward project, which used the money to fund the purchase of motorised wheelchairs 'which would increase the mobility of young people with special needs'. A massive campaign was run over just one weekend (from Thursday, 31 October to Saturday, 2 November). Through the IGG's efforts, thirty-seven wheelchairs were purchased.

As Guiding in Ireland celebrated its eightieth birthday in 1991, a National Camp was organised at the Cistercian Abbey of Mount Melleray. The camp was opened by the Minister of State for the Environment, Mary Harney TD, on 20 July 1991. It was, according to the *Irish Times*, 'the biggest camp for girls ever held in Ireland'. Over 1,200 Irish Guides attended, along with a large contingent from the Catholic Guides of Ireland and international Guides from Belgium, France, Greece, Czechoslovakia, the United Kingdom, Northern Ireland, Australia, New Zealand, Canada and Japan, while a non-Guide group of girls from Chernobyl also attended. According to the *Irish Times*, 'The Abbot of Mount Melleray, Dom. Eamonn Fitzgerald, and the Church of Ireland Dean of Lismore, the Very Rev. Cecil Weekes, blessed the flags of the participating nations at a special opening ceremony'. Linda White, a Guider from Canada, wrote about her time at the camp:

> The girls exchanged thoughts and concerns with girls from other countries. Freedom was talked about with the girls from Czechoslovakia. Culture and dances were shared with the leader from Greece. Peace and unity were hoped for with the girls from Northern Ireland. Looking out over a campsite (even if it is a little muddy!), with so many nations living together in friendship and happiness, I'm sure would plant a wish for world peace in each heart of the Canadian delegation. Such an experience (the first time for many) will end with each girl trying in whatever small way she can to make such a wish come true.
>
> *The Canadian Guider Magazine*

Mary Harney addresses Mellary, 1991. (Courtesy of the Irish Examiner)

A review of the Guide uniform was undertaken in the early 1990s, as it was felt that the uniform was old-fashioned and impractical. After consultation with the Guide units around the country, and following a survey which weighed up the problems girls had with their uniform, it was decided to launch a new uniform – which, for the first time, featured a degree of choice within its design. Some Guides wanted to change to a more informal style of uniform, which would

Previous: *Aerial photo of Mellary 1991.*

Members modelling the IGG uniform worn before the review in the early 1990s.

Senior Branch members and Guiders modelling the new uniform in the early 1990s.

include jeans and sweatshirts, while others preferred a blouse and skirt. All these choices were incorporated into the new style: Now, for the first time in eighty years, Guides could be seen sporting jeans or navy trousers, while Rangers adopted a green sweatshirt with a red polo shirt.

Standing camps were introduced in 1992. These camps are already up and ready to go when participants arrive, which means that campers do not need to worry about putting up or taking down tents, and have more time to enjoy the activities which are on offer. This arrangement also allowed children whose leaders didn't have the required qualifications to bring them away overnight, to camp. More than three hundred Guides took part in these camps, which were held in four regions throughout the summer. Each camp was staffed by two qualified Guiders and eight Rangers/Young Leaders, for whom the camps provided a summer job. The girls were on site for periods of three days to experience a taste of camping, and a programme of varied outdoor activities was also on offer. In October 1992, *Trefoil News* reported:

> The backbone of these camps was eight friendly, competent Young Guiders. . . . They ran games and campfires, organised the central cooking, manned the First Aid tent, organised the Patrols and duties and were always available for the Guides. Everyone who participated in these camps agreed that they were a great success and hope that they will be repeated next year.

—◌◌◌—

A major change in the administration of Guiding in Ireland and Ireland's relationship with WAGGGS took place in 1992. According to the rules of the World Association of Girl Guides and Girl Scouts, each member country can only be represented by one national organisation. The Catholic Guides of Ireland were not members of WAGGGS and could not attend events organised by the World Association. In the 1970s, the CGI expressed a wish to become members of WAGGGS. Over the following twenty years, discussions were ongoing about finding a way to allow CGI to become more involved in international Guiding. The IGG and the CGI, with assistance from the World Board (which governs WAGGGS), worked together on this, and in December 1992 it was agreed to establish Comhairle Bantreoraithe na hÉireann – the Council of Irish Guiding Associations (CIGA) – an umbrella organisation to incorporate both associations as one member of WAGGGS. CIGA consists of the Irish Girl Guides and the Catholic Guides of Ireland, on behalf of their members resident in the Republic of Ireland (the CGI has members in both the Republic and Northern Ireland). The CIGI committee is made up of four members of the IGG and four members of the Catholic Guides of Ireland from the Republic; there are two members of CGI from Northern Ireland as observers, and two members of the Girlguiding Ulster as visitors. At the twenty-eighth world conference in 1993, CIGA was ratified as a full member of the World Association of Girl Guides and Girl Scouts, and was recognised as continuing the full membership for Ireland, which was first gained by the Irish Girl Guides in 1932.

Georgia – Ireland – Georgia Link pamphlet.

Although both WAGGGS and individual national organisations are apolitical, the change in political landscapes and geographical boundaries affected them. The fall of the Berlin Wall in 1989 changed the face of Europe. The liberalisation of the Bloc's authoritarian systems led to an opening up of the Eastern Bloc; as a result, new countries were opened up to Western culture, media and organisations. Following the break-up of the former Soviet Union, WAGGGS made moves to link the former Soviet countries with Western countries. The aim was to empower each new country to set up its own Guide association, with material support and training to enable it to gain access to the mainstream of European Guiding. Ireland was chosen as the link country for Georgia, and over the following years

Guiders from CGI and IGG celebrate the ratification of the Council of Guiding Associations (CIGA) in 1993.

training events, visits and joint camps were planned. The US state of Georgia agreed to back Ireland in its work with the country. Thus began a three-way Georgia–Ireland–Georgia link. The western European countries stood to play a crucial role in the development of Guiding and Scouting in the newly emerging republics in Eastern Europe. The introduction of the concept of non-political voluntary organisations, managed from within, with their own structure, constitution and programme, was a refreshing and previously unheard of experience for the young people of these former Communist countries.

There were numerous visits to Georgia by Irish Guiders from 1993 to 2001. These included large groups and individual trainers: one member, Jan Bartlett, actually lived there for several months. (Jan, who passed away in 1998, was recognised for her work in Georgia at the 1999 world conference). The first trainer to travel from Ireland was Vanessa Wyse Jackson, who went to Georgia as part of a WAGGGS delegation in 1993. They spoke with the new Georgian Girl Scout Association ('Dia') and were able to assess their training and practical needs. They also did some basic training with a group of twenty-five potential leaders. Groups of leaders from Georgia also visited Ireland and had the opportunity to visit units around the country, work with regional development officers and visit other youth organisations. Joy Clarke, a trainer sent by the Irish Girl Guides to Georgia, recalls:

> The Georgian people were so kind and generous to us. [Their attitude was] 'Visitors were a gift from God'. The leaders that we trained, both boys and girls, were very eager to learn about Guiding, and we managed very well using interpreters and a lot of practical demonstrations.

—◦◦◦—

For younger members of the IGG, there was a Georgia Link Badge which, through its syllabus, created awareness of the country amongst the members; a large numbers of girls around the country did the badge. Units all over the country, keen to support the new movement in Georgia, undertook to raise funds to provide 'Dia' with resources to continue its exiting work. As Vanessa Wyse Jackson relates, a group of Georgian Guides and Scouts visited Ireland in 1994:

> In July 1994, a hugely significant staging post on the 'link road', was when a group of thirteen Georgian Guides and Scouts arrived in Ireland to take part in a camp in County Kilkenny with some Irish Guides and Scouts and a delegation of Girl Scouts from Georgia in the United States. From there, the Georgians travelled to an international jamboree in Wales and were able to experience being part of a world movement at first hand.

—◦◦◦—

In the late 1990s, as the political situation in the Caucasus became more unstable, an appeal was launched. Guides from all over Ireland responded with generosity and, as Vanessa Wyse Jackson reports: 'IGG was able to build further on its experience and team up with UNHCR to provide peace packs for Georgian refugee children affected by the unrest'.

Service projects also took place in Georgia in the late 1990s. Helen Concannon from Barna, a member of one of the projects, remembers:

> The Georgia link gave IGG an opportunity to 'live' the Guiding ethos and develop lasting friendships and a real sense of sisterhood. By

working with 'Dia' on the development of their organisation, IGG gained experienced, skilled, creative leaders through the service projects and exchange programmes. Working with refugee children in remote parts of Georgia gave IGG Senior Branch members a mind-blowing, humbling experience. Having the Georgian leaders visit Ireland gave IGG members around the country a chance to learn about each other's countries. IGG units were privileged to experience the Georgian culture of music, singing and dancing with Georgian Girl Guide Leaders.

At the WAGGGS world conference in 1999 (hosted in Dublin), Georgia was awarded associate membership of the World Association. Diane Dixon, international commissioner (1995-2001), notes:

> It was a highlight for IGG and all the work put into the link. Starting from the beginning, it was fascinating to watch the Georgians absorb so much of the methods of Guiding and their interest and questions as to why things were done and the methods we used. It also made us question sometimes why we did things and how we did them.

Cheerful Girl Scouts in the Republic of Georgia.

At the same conference, the IGG was awarded a WAGGGS UNHCR Award for service projects in the Republic of Georgia. In the same year, the IGG was also awarded a gold Gulbenkian Citizenship Award. Linda Peters, international commissioner (1989-1995), recalls:

> Looking at this link [with Georgia] in the family context, we are privileged to have been involved in the birth of Guiding in Georgia, and will do our best to give the support and training necessary for the successful growth of our sister organisation. We cannot do this without the help of our support link – the 'twin-sister' state of Georgia, USA, not to mention the maternal help of WAGGGS!

⌐∾∾⌐

The link with Georgia was the biggest and most long-term project the IGG had ever undertaken. It was also one of the greatest successes in the history of the IGG.

Work was begun in 1993 on an extension to Guide headquarters in 27 Pembroke Park, with the work set to give HQ an extra room for meetings, a new bedroom, and additional toilet and storage space. Meanwhile, major work was also being done on the Guide cottage in Enniskerry, with the donation of a third of an acre by the Slazenger family (owners of the Powerscourt estate since 1961) providing land in which the buses carrying Brownies and Guides could park.

The Brownie uniform was changed in 1993 to a yellow sweatshirt and T-shirt, navy tracksuit bottoms or culottes, and a navy neckerchief and badge sash. Brownies continued their fun adventures and loved to earn badges for their sashes. Sarah Browne, a member of Bennett Brownies and St Ciaran's Guides in Athlone in the 1990s, remembers:

> The best days of my life were at Brownies in St Mary's Hall in Athlone. There was always a different adventure every week, whether we were

going to the old monastery, out in Portlick for cooking competitions, or just meeting our friends and having fun. We loved our sashes, and it was great fun trying to collect as many badges as we could. Then we went on to the Guides, which was fun as well, with little adventures here and there, and exploring the surrounding area. The best thing was helping with the Ladybirds and teaching them what I knew about exploring, and showing them how to be good Ladybirds.

——◦◊◦——

Brownies and their leaders with Mairéad McGuinness at the opening of the North East premises.

After the introduction of the new uniform, a collection of old uniforms was held; the world bureau advised that Mauritania would welcome as many uniforms as could be sent. While the Brownies changed their uniform, Guides were taking part in trips on the *Asgard* and the *Queen Galadriel* sailing ships. Both ships were training vessels which were used to train young people in sailing techniques and presented a unique opportunity for members of the Irish Girl Guides to meet new people and have life-changing experiences onboard.

In the same year, the Olave Baden-Powell Society asked if it could hold its 1994 ceremony in Ireland. The Olave Baden-Powell

Society is a global group of people who choose to support the development of girls and young women. The Society raises funds for the World Association of Girl Guides and Girl Scouts, which through its 140-plus member countries and 10 million-plus members, demonstrates and delivers democratic processes for girls and young women, including programmes relating to adolescent health, literacy, and safe food and water. Membership is sought by several different types of people, both Guiding and non-Guiding, male and female. The Olave Baden-Powell Society focuses on the development of girls and young women. This was to be the first official event hosted by the newly formed CIGA and was attended by a total of seventy members from fifteen countries. At the meeting in Dublin, Margaret Hamilton-Reid (international commissioner, 1956–70) joined Frances Dwyer, a former chief commissioner and national president, as the IGG members of the society.

The Senior Branch launched their new magazine in 1995. The *Welly* began life as a quarterly magazine which was an alternative to *Trefoil News* for younger members of the association. It advertised Senior Branch events and contained articles written by Senior Branchers who had attended events and wanted to share their experiences with others. It is now produced bi-annually. Ollie Ballantine recalls the early days of the magazine:

> I really don't know what possessed us, or how we thought that there were a few empty hours in our day

Two guides entertaining at the Olave Baden-Powell Society event.

that needed filling, but somehow, somebody decided that Senior Branch should have their own magazine. And somewhere along the line, it fell to us [Maria Kidney and Ollie Ballantine] to create this tome of wisdom.

⁓

With the peace talks building to what would become the historic Good Friday Agreement in Northern Ireland, the six Guiding and Scouting Associations on the island of Ireland chose peace as their theme for the year. The six associations were the Catholic Boy Scouts of Ireland, the Irish Girl Guides, the Scout Association of Ireland, the Scouting Association of Northern Ireland, the Girl Guide Association, Northern Ireland, and the Catholic Guides of Ireland. The three Guiding Associations were part of a 'peace pack' initiative: in December 1995, 3,343 peace packs left Dublin on their journey to Georgia. The packs included personal-hygiene products and stationery, which were to be given to refugee children. During May 1996, the packs were distributed by representatives of the UN High Commissioner for Refugees and Jan Bartlett. A joint committee was put together, and they produced an activity pack that was used by all age groups in all six associations. The pack was designed to encourage young people to become aware of the many aspects of peace, and the importance and benefits of it. It was hoped that by the end of the year, the members of all the associations would feel that peace was something that touched all aspects of their daily lives. Units were encouraged to take part in a peace walk throughout Ireland, joining a unit from another Guide or Scout organisation in their area. The peace committee organised design competitions for peace posters and T-shirts; both attracted many entries. Throughout 1996, the theme of peace was developed, and a total of 4,092 peace badges were earned during the year, showing the educational benefit of this theme.

The chief event for the 'Year of Peace' was the International Camp, Campa Cáirde, meaning 'Peace through Friendship', which was held at Ballyfin College, Portlaoise. There were around a thousand campers: groups from ten different countries – Australia, Canada, USA, Germany, France, New Zealand, Ulster, Scotland, the United Kingdom and Wales – travelled to Ireland for the event. The

IGG and CGI Guides packing peace packs for Georgia.

Opposite:
Senior Branch trip to Rome.

Preparing dinner on Campa Cháirde, 1996.

activities were based on the theme of peace but were certainly not always peaceful! Activities included archery; completing an assault course; abseiling; canoeing; rafting; swimming; pioneering; orienteering; hill walking; overnight survival; set dancing; water and shelter aid; food and transport aid; and crafts. A peace fair was held, and funds were raised in aid of Georgia. There was also an international night, at which all the international Guides participated, and a '60s night, with 'flower power' costumes and peace make-up. The 'Purple Durples' were the service team for the camp; many who served on this team went on to become committed Guiders and are still members of the organisation. Hazel Convery, the Camp Chief, remembers:

A new 'Section' of IGG came into being at the camp. This was the 'Purple Durples', the name adopted by the service team for the camp, made up of members of IGG's Senior Branch, Venture Scouts and some international visitors. No effort was spared in producing a 'purple atmosphere', from their own flag, to purple violets decorating their campsite, not forgetting their purple neckerchiefs. However, these efforts were matched by the enthusiasm and work that they put into all the jobs assigned to them, in particular the running of all the activities. We hear on the grapevine that they will be the 'Mellow Yellows' next time.

Senior Branchers arriving into camp.

—◦◦◦◦—

An ad hoc committee was set up to review the Guide Law. The wording of the Guide Law, which encapsulates the ethos of the movement, had remained unchanged since 1911. Questionnaires were sent to all leaders during the year, and their opinions and suggestions were taken into account when making the changes. In 1996, the executive committee approved the changes to the law.

In May 1996, Linda Peters, former international commissioner, was appointed chief executive officer. She was the first person to hold this new title: the job which she was undertaking had previously been known as 'secretary general'. This job had been held by Kitty Richardson for twenty-two years, until her retirement. When Kitty died in 1997, it was noted in *Trefoil News* that:

> So many of us, young and old, remember the happy times we spent
> at camp with Kitty. In rain or shine she was always the same smiling,
> cheerful Kitty.

—◦◦◦◦—

The IGG introduced its first Code of Ethics and Good Practice in 1997 – the first youth organisation in Ireland to do so. The code was launched by Jillian Hassett (later Jillian van Turnhout), president of the National Youth Council of Ireland. The new code, which was published in booklet form, clearly set out the aims and objectives of the IGG. It included information on, and definitions of, child abuse, emotional abuse, neglect, sexual abuse and bullying, and guidelines on how to respond to suspected child abuse. As a voluntary organisation working with children, the IGG does everything in its power to ensure that the children in its care are protected from harm. In 1997, Hazel Convery became chief

*Chief Commissioner
Hazel Convery
presenting awards
to participants.*

commissioner. Her predecessor, Margaret Dunne, had completed seven years in the position and noted upon her retirement:

> National events have been documented in the annual reports but no report can truly reflect the enthusiasm, dedication and ability of those who work with our young people or who spend many hours travelling to meetings to make plans for our association. . . . In an age where so much importance is put on measurable achievement, and integrity and moral values often take a back seat, it is more important than ever that we ensure that as many girls and young women as possible can benefit from Guiding.

In 1997, the IGG introduced its mission statement: 'The mission of the Irish Girl Guides is to enable girls and young women to develop to their fullest potential as responsible citizens of the world'. Following the introduction of the mission statement, a website was launched in 1998. Guiding in Ireland was embracing new technology and striving to make the association more accessible.

In the spirit of modernisation, and in an effort to maintain membership numbers, a programme review committee had been formed. This committee was given the brief to produce a user-friendly programme with radical new ideas. In 1998, new programmes for Guides and Brownies were introduced. This was the first comprehensive overhaul of the programmes that had taken place since the early twentieth century. The awards themselves still bore the names (first class, second class, etc) that had been given to them by the Baden-Powells, and they had the same basic structure, but they were now called Footprints for Brownies and Trees for Guides. Previously, each child had to complete every part of the programme in order to progress to the next part; the new programmes introduced an element of choice and also meant that girls joining the unit could slot into their appropriate age group and work with their peers. The programme was more flexible, allowed the girls to have more control over their goals, and gave them more responsibility within the unit. For the first time, the programme was available in one place. (Booklets were put together for the girls, and activity folders for the leaders.) Activity packs for each level were also introduced, to make planning meetings much easier for busy volunteers. Everything was done in an attempt to make life easier for volunteers, to hold the interest of the girls, and to continue to develop the movement.

The Irish Girl Guides had adopted the WAGGGS 'Building World Citizenship' theme for the Guiding year starting in September 1998. Through a variety of activities and events, the IGG aimed to raise awareness of world citizenship in the lead-up to the thirtieth world conference, which was due to be held in Dublin. Activity packs were produced for each of the four branches in co-operation with DEFY (Development Education for Youth). WAGGGS identified a number of themes: culture and heritage, health, environment, education, peace and food, and nutrition. The IGG chose to focus on education. The packs were divided into four

Ray Darcy taking part in a merchandising campaign.

sections: 'Me, Myself'; 'Me and Others'; 'Myself within a Wider World'; and 'Human Rights'. In 1999, Ladybirds marked their tenth anniversary. To celebrate, Rainbow Guides (Ulster) and Cygnets (CGI) joined 1,500 Ladybird Guides and more than four hundred Guiders and parents at parties all over Ireland.

In 1999, the Irish Girl Guides started an association with Operation Christmas Child, an initiative of Samaritan's Purse, a Christian relief and development agency working amongst communities in need in eighteen countries across Africa, eastern Europe and central Asia. Operation Christmas Child works with various organisations to send shoeboxes full of gifts and essentials to children in developing countries. Units from as far afield as Valentia Island and Donegal took part in the project as their Christmas Good Turn. Ladybirds, Brownies and Guides filled almost 2,000 shoeboxes with items such as confectionary, toys, games, stationery, books and clothing. In all, 35,000 boxes were sent from Ireland in four lorry-loads: two travelled to Romania, and one each went to Poland and Serbia.

The 1990s had been good to Ireland. According to Diarmaid Ferriter: 'from 1987 until the end of the century economic growth (GNP) averaged over 5 percent, while in some years, growth was over 10 percent. In a single decade, the growth in employment stood at 20 percent, and between 1987 and 2003 unemployment fell from 17 to 4 percent. The boom was a result of a switch to a directed approach on economic policy on the part of government, competitive corporation taxes, greater access to third-level education, more participation by married women in the

Ladybirds celebrate their birthday.

Opposite: One of the many Brownie units who packed and sent shoeboxes with Samaritan's Purse.

workforce (53 percent of married women were working by 2006, compared to 8 percent in 1971) and social partnerships between governments and trade unions. By 1997, nearly half of all manufacturing jobs were in foreign-owned companies, illustrating the importance of a growth-orientated approach, helped by EU funding, but also the significance of the education initiatives of the 1960s'.†

† *Ireland in the Twentieth Century*

The Irish Girl Guides benefited from this boom, with increased funding which helped to keep membership numbers steady. The end of the millennium was approaching fast, and Irish Guiding was going to end it with a bang. CIGA was determined that the WAGGGS world conference in University College Dublin would be an event to remember.

CHAPTER 9

The World Conference and a New Century

The WAGGGS world conference meets every three years to decide the overall strategy for Girl Guiding and Girl Scouting for the coming three years. CIGA bid for the privilege of hosting the WAGGGS world conference in 1999 at the world conference in Canada in 1996. The bid was successful, and for the following three years intensive work was done by both associations to prepare for the event. Hosting the 1999 event was a unique opportunity for Irish Guiding to showcase its talents and international prowess. This massive undertaking was organised by a core committee chaired by Elspeth Henderson, eight subcommittees, and an administrator. Elspeth recalls:

> Little could I have anticipated that Ireland would be hosting the WAGGGS world conference in 1999 and that I would be chairing the planning team at that event, thirty-five years later [after working at her first international event in 1965]! On a much larger scale, the world

Opposite: *IGG uniforms past and present. (Courtesy of the Irish Times)*

World Conference logo.

conference mirrored my experience of that earlier event. In both instances, the 'business' had to be done, but my abiding memory is of the fun, energy and commitment of the delegates. I felt privileged to be a member of the 'world family' of Guiding.

For two years prior to the conference, the committees worked with enthusiasm to ensure that the event would be remembered with pleasure and would showcase the talents of Irish Guiding. It was an exciting time for CIGA, and a massive opportunity for the associations to work together. The theme of the conference was 'Dream, Dare, Do'. An Irish Guider, Ollie Ballantine, wrote a song, 'Dare to Dream', to reflect the theme. The chorus of the song ran:

> *No matter what our colour, creed or country,*
> *We'll share a dream of how it's going to be.*
> *We'll bring it home to teach to those around us,*
> *And do you dare to turn your dream into reality?*

One Brownie, who was chosen to dance in the opening ceremony, Emma Harvey of Ballybrack Guides, remembers:

Eventually the big night came along and everyone was nervous backstage. We were dressed in our costumes and I was amazed at the dresses worn by the older girls who were doing Irish dancing. . . . My friends and I could hardly contain our excitement and kept peeking out from behind the curtain and trying to see what was going on. At last it was our turn to go on, and we danced our hearts out with the biggest grins on our faces. During my second dance, I caught sight of my parents and waved. Unfortunately, as I waved to them and they waved back, this was the only time the camera was on me. Everyone in the audience let out an audible 'aww' as the smallest girl on stage seemed to wave at them all with a giant smile.

—◦◦◦—

Activities at Camp Aisling, 1999.

In conjunction with the conference, a camp for members of the IGG, the CGI and the Guide Association (Province of Ulster), and organised by CIGA, was held in the grounds of the university. Marg McInerney (from Carrigaline), the Camp Chief, remembers the problems with organising such a large and prestigious camp, and also the logistics of drawing together such a geographically diverse committee:

This camp provided me with many challenging moments. With three associations involved from very opposite ends of the country, we used some, for the time, very innovative solutions. To avoid travelling and to save money, we used a three-way call facility to organise much of the camp. The theme of the camp was 'Dream, Dare, Do', and the activities reflected these ideas.

One of the special moments for me was seeing the world conference delegates wander into the

campsite in the evening time to visit the Guides. This brought it home
to the Guides what a truly international movement we belonged to.

—◦◊◦—

Over the ten days of the conference and camp, the excitement never waned. More
than five hundred women from 136 countries took part. This was a major
showcase of Ireland, and an opportunity for the 'world' to visit. The conference
brought home to Irish Guides the truly international strength and diversity of
the world association. Many people who had not been involved with Guiding for
many years came back into the fold, and many who are still involved with the
movement list this event as one of the highlights of their time in Guiding.

Following the excitement of the world conference, there was a renewed vigour
and excitement within the association, and as the world entered the new
millennium the IGG felt that this milestone should not pass without some
celebration. On 19 February 2000, four hundred Guiders arrived at the Grand
Hotel in Malahide to celebrate the past, present and future of Guiding. There were
Guiders from every branch, commissioners, and members of Trefoil Guild present.
Participants explored the highs of Guiding over the past twenty years, thought
about Guiding in the present, and listened to the keynote speaker, John Lonergan,
governor of Mountjoy Prison. The day closed with a Thinking Day service.

As always, the Irish Girl Guides were striving to raise awareness of the plight
of those living in the developing world: in 2001, Sahan Resource Pack was
created by the IGG in conjunction with Trócaire. The aim of this joint project
was to raise awareness amongst members of the situation and living conditions
for women in countries like Somalia. The packs were developed for each age
group within the organisation and were widely utilised by units countrywide;

those who completed the activities were awarded a badge. On 27 February, the *Irish Times* reported:

> Sahan, two activity packs on life in Somalia produced by the Irish Girl Guides and Trócaire, artfully impart all sorts of information about the living conditions of girls and women in Somalia. The junior pack is for five- to ten-year-olds, the senior for those aged ten and over. As well as activity sheets, the packs include information sheets for adult leaders on conditions in Somalia, a poster, and a cassette with songs, music, language, drumbeats and more.

A new chief commissioner, Jillian van Turnhout, was appointed in 2001. She reflected, in *Trefoil News*, on her first year in her new post:

> My first year as chief commissioner has given me many challenges and opportunities. My highlight will always be meeting with our members throughout the country, seeing the work they are doing, in playing their role towards the education of girls and young women.

Also in 2001, the Irish Girl Guides celebrated ninety years of Guiding. In September, a birthday banquet, which was held in conjunction with the national Conference, was attended by members, past and present, from all over Ireland, all with different experiences and memories. Jillian van Turnhout remarked that:

> Ninety years ago the first official Guide Company was set up in Harold's Cross, with Guiding spreading to all ends of the country by

Recipients of the Ireland InVOLved Awards 2001.

1920. Since this time we have had many highs, and some lows. However, throughout we have ensured that the fundamental principles of Duty to God, Duty to Country and Service to the Community are the foundation of Guiding. We have carried on the Spirit of Guiding so that its flame still burns brightly.

※

The Irish Girl Guides celebrated the United Nations International Year of Volunteers (IYV) in a variety of ways. In January 2001, a thank-you card was sent to the support team/family behind every one of the volunteer leaders; volunteer pins bearing the IYV logo were launched at the General Council meeting and subsequently posted to each of our leaders. Car stickers bearing the slogan 'Guiding supports our volunteers' were also sent to each leader during the year.

The highlight of the IYV came in December, when several leaders were nominated for the Ireland *InVOLved* Awards. The IGG received an award as a volunteer-friendly organisation. Two adult leaders, Maura Fitzgerald and Lydia Nesbitt, received awards in the Volunteering Impact category, and Lydia was presented with the top award in this category by President McAleese.

The outbreak of foot and mouth disease in the same year meant that all Guiding activities throughout the country had to be suspended for more than three weeks in March. At the end of March, the suspension on meetings was lifted. The ban on all outdoor activities continued, however, and most IGG outdoor centres remained closed until mid-April. In mid-May, restrictions on activities such as hill-walking were lifted and the remaining outdoor centres reopened.

The foot and mouth crisis did not stop members of the Irish Girl Guides from selling thousands of mince pies on behalf of the CREW network, as their Christmas Good Turn. The CREW Network was founded in 1996 to address the problem of substance misuse in a person-centred way through education programmes. The aim of the network was to assist in the achievement of learning outcomes for health promotion, drug education and citizenship through the delivery of programmes that support best practice in primary drug education and as an integral part of the government's National Drugs Strategy.

In 2002, it was time for another international event – and another chance to showcase Ireland – when Solas International Camp was held in Charleville, County Cork. In all, 1,100 Guides and leaders from numerous countries attended: there were participants from Bermuda, Denmark, England, Scotland, Wales, Northern Ireland, USA, Germany, France, Taiwan, France, St Vincent and the Grenadines, the Bahamas, and New Zealand. The sun shone on the camp during what was otherwise a very wet summer. Activities ranged from the adventurous to the educational to the silly-but-fun. Jenny Gannon from Newbridge recalls:

> I never made it to an International Camp as a Guide but in 2002 I headed to my first, Camp Solas, as a grown-up. As I wandered through the campsite one morning it really was a sight to behold: a town which had sprung up overnight, the office busy with computers and people typing away, outside there was a group doing some t'ai chi, kiddies in the crèche painting pictures, leaders having a welcome catch-up in the coffee shop while next door the central catering team were busy

preparing lunch for the activity staff, and the supermarket staff counting and distributing the five hundred burgers due out that day. The shouts of girls in the distance and squeals of laughter from the obstacle course and the craft tent reminded us all of why we were here.

——◦◦◦◦——

Jemma Lee from Athlone also attended the camp:

Girls learning about Harambee project.

I remember feeling completely overwhelmed by the whole scale of the camp. There were people everywhere! So many different kinds of tents, all the different accents, and lots of work to do! I was on the activity-staff team, and our first task was the opening ceremony and campfire. We helped to light up an entire field of candles and then marched with torches to the fire and set it ablaze. It was just magical.

——◦◦◦◦——

Throughout 2002, all members were part of a Kenyan awareness initiative, called 'Harambee'. The focal point of the 'Harambee' project saw a group of Irish leaders, from the IGG, CGI and Girlguiding Ulster (the Ulster Association was renamed in 2002 in line with the rebranding of the UK association), go to Kenya and participate in a service project in Bethel Children's Home in Londiani. The development-education programme saw members throughout Ireland learn more about life in Kenya and then go on to collect many items and raise funds for Bethel. During their three-week stay in Kenya, members of the team took part in a wide range of activities – running a summer camp for the children from the home, painting chairs, planting trees, repairing clothes, helping the children with their English, and reading and introducing an AIDS/HIV awareness programme to women from the local village. Although only fourteen members travelled to Kenya, many more took part in other ways: by raising funds or collecting equipment to be sent to Kenya, by taking part in the awareness campaign and earning the Harambee badge, and by having a participant speak and show slides of the project to them on their return to Kenya. Following this project, a number of the people who had been involved in the service project went on to found an independent charity, Friends of Londiani, which has five members of the IGG – Maria Kidney, Helen Concannon, Hazel Murphy, Deirdre Henley and, more recently, Maebh Ní Bhúinneáin – on its board of directors. Catherine O'Connor from Thurles remembers:

One of the volunteers working with one of the children in Bethel.

Volunteers on the Harambee project in Kenya visit Lord Baden-Powell's grave.

Early in 2001 when I heard there was a service project possibly going to take place in Kenya with members of IGG and possibly CGI and GG Ulster, I was so excited by the idea. The idea that through the world of Guiding a link could be created and developed, which gave opportunities to girls, young women and adults in both parts of the world to grow and develop in different ways to help reach their fullest potential. . . . From this initial project, it is wonderful to see that through lots of hard work the registered charity, Friends of Londiani, Ireland, has emerged and has continued to grow from strength to strength and make a real difference since the Guiding service project in 2002.

———✂✄——

The Irish Girl Guides began to explore the concept of spirituality within their programme and how to better apply it to the everyday running of the organisation. In 2003, Maria Kidney, a leader from Cobh, travelled to the Ehecatl spirituality workshop run by WAGGGS in Our Cabaña, Mexico. As a result of this workshop, a team was formed to look at spirituality within the IGG. This team explored the programme of the Irish Girl Guides to see where spirituality already existed and where the WAGGGS pack on spirituality was being utilised, and to identify the gaps between the two. In an effort to increase awareness of spirituality within the association, the team organised ceremonies at the national conference, branch weekends and regional conferences, and organised a spirituality workshop in 2004. Over the following few years, they published articles on the subject in *Trefoil News*, produced a CD for those planning a Guides' Own (a planned time of reflection with a spiritual element), developed resources on the Promise and Law, and continued to contribute to ceremonies, Guides' Owns, and activities run at regional and national events.

In 2004, the IGG was awarded the Gold Health Quality Mark by the National Youth Health Programme in recognition of its ethos, policy and practice as a quality health-promoting organisation. It was the first national organisation to gain the Gold Health Quality Mark and has maintained it ever since. That summer, in conjunction with the Samaritan's Purse charity, twenty leaders took part in a service project in Hungary for two weeks in August, during which time they ran a summer camp for thirty-one disadvantaged children from Serbia. The Irish contingent was responsible for the daily programme, which included spirituality sessions, crafts, songs, games and sports.

Guiding continued to embrace development education (which aims to deepen understanding of global poverty and encourage people towards action for a more just and equal world); in an effort to develop a better understanding of the wider world for older girls and leaders, a national day was planned. The largest national event of the year was Dance to a Different Beat, a development-education day held in Newbridge, County Kildare. This event gave five hundred Guides and leaders an opportunity to take part in a wide range of activities related to development education. Fun activities included tribal drumming, salsa, Greek and Irish dancing, making dream-catchers and learning about international Guiding. Workshops were held on One World Week, Building World Citizenship, refugees, HIV/AIDS, spirituality and the environment.

Senior Branchers planning a Guides' Own.

Samaritan's Purse Camp.

Lisa Concannon from Galway attended the event in Newbridge:

It was amazing to see five hundred girls all together and see how enthusiastic and willing to learn they were. It gave a great sense of togetherness and showed the true Girl Guide spirit.

———

In the same year, a new competition, 'Timpeall an Domhain' ('Around the World'), was run by the International Committee for all Guide units. It encouraged Guides to learn about other countries and cultures. Patrols of Guides had to choose countries from a list of ten and then undertake challenges related to each country: e.g. cook a traditional meal, prepare a display, create a traditional costume, and demonstrate a craft. This competition prompted girls to consider the international nature of Guiding and allowed them to experience other cultures while having fun with their friends.

In 2004 and 2005, the IGG was centre-stage internationally, with two Irish leaders, Diane Dixon and Elspeth Henderson, being elected to high-ranking positions. In 2004, at the WAGGGS European Conference, Diane was elected as chairman of the Europe Committee, and in 2005 Elspeth was elected chairman of the WAGGGS World Board. In terms of World Guiding, Ireland is a relatively small Guiding organisation: to be so well represented and respected at world level is recognition of members' hard work and diligence over the years.

As society became more litigious, with increasing focus on child welfare and the protection of the volunteer, the concept of reporting officers (people who dealt with disputes and complaints within the IGG and reported back to the association) was introduced. These officers help resolve a dispute that cannot be solved by the parties involved. Fortunately, to date there has been very little need for these skilled officers to be used.

In 2005, the IGG branched out into the wider society and engaged with the social changes of modern Ireland. Traditionally, Ireland has been a country marked by a declining population and high rates of emigration, but this situation changed since the mid-1990s, and immigration increased significantly in the context of rapid economic growth. At first, flows were driven by returning Irish emigrants, but from the early 2000s non-EU nationals began to arrive in significant numbers for the first time, mainly to work but also to seek asylum. The scale of these developments put Irish policy-makers under pressure, and the response was often ad hoc. Integration became a hot topic at all levels, including youth movements. Government funding was secured by the IGG for an outreach project. This once-off grant enabled the association to develop the work it was already doing with the Travelling community and to initiate cooperation with asylum-seekers and refugees. An outreach development officer was employed to help raise members' awareness of the challenges faced by the target groups in Ireland and to support the leaders in adapting the Guiding programme to the needs of the targeted groups. A pilot project was a summer camp in Corduff, in 2006; girls from all backgrounds were encouraged to attend, and girls from the Travelling community, Africa, Eastern Europe and Asia took part, along with Brownies and Guides from Corduff.

The Irish Girl Guides have always rallied in the face of any local, national or international disaster. They were on hand during the two world wars, the War of Independence and the civil war, picking up the pieces in post-war Europe, helping the poor, raising money for charities operating at home and abroad, and working

Girls participating in the Corduff Outreach Project.

in Georgia, Kenya, Hungary and many other countries. In more recent times, when Hurricane Katrina struck or the tsunami devastated Thailand, the IGG was on hand to do what they could by raising money, increasing awareness, and sending essential goods to stricken areas. Service to the community has always been an integral part of the Guiding programme and is an important value that is instilled in all members.

Camping and outdoor activities have long been associated with Guiding and Scouting alike. The girls have never shied away from the harder side of the outdoor life, and from the moment they were allowed under canvas and into the wilderness, they never wanted to come home. The equipment we have available today may be far more advanced than what was available in the early twentieth century but, perhaps surprisingly, the fundamentals of Girl Guide camping have not changed that much. As we have seen, in 1984 three Rangers from Cork had been the first IGG team to participate in the Explorer Belt in Sweden. In 2006, the Explorer Belt

Enjoying ice cream at Corduff Outreach Project.

returned to Sweden for another historic occasion – the first IGG-run Belt. Two teams of two members each took part, and all had the time of their lives. High on a cliff top at Ales Stenar, at a Viking stone monument shaped like a ship, a short ceremony was held to present the belts and certificates. Rose Hennessy, who had been part of the first IGG team to take part in the expedition in 1984, made the presentation to the teams.

The Guiding highlight of 2007 was the international camp at Campa Le Chéile in Ratoath, County Meath. The camp was preceded by the Chief Commissioners Award, which was plagued by bad weather (as was the international camp itself). The theme of the camp was 'Celebrating Cultural Diversity': international visitors from as far afield as Australia, New Zealand, Canada, South Africa, Nigeria, Kenya, Singapore, USA and the Philippines joined Irish Guides for a week of activities. Although it seemed that the rain never

The 2006 Explorer Belt participants meet the chairman of the World Board, Elspeth Henderson.

stopped, the thousand-strong crew of Irish girls and their visitors had an action-packed week of fun and friendship. The sun shone for visitors' day, where each camp hosted an activity to raise funds for charity: €4,000 was raised for VAMOS!, a children's organisation in Mexico, and ChildLine. The activities included bouncing castles and trampolines, fishing, overnight survival, camogie, crafts, UNHCR and outreach tents, spirituality, outdoor cooking, dance, pioneering and a disco. There were also day trips to Dublin, the bog, Drogheda and Trim. Jenna Goodwin from Lucan recalls:

I remember Campa Le Chéile when I was on activity staff. Everyone on camp got to go on a day out to Dublin during the week, even activity staff. So halfway through the week we decided to go on the Viking Splash Tour and then to the National Aquatic Centre. So we packed up our togs and our towels that morning and were very excited. . . . We arrived at the NAC and we all threw on our togs and headed straight for the showers! Never mind about the slides and the wave pool, it was the showers that we were interested in. And it was the nicest shower I've ever had!

A new Guiding event was held in September 2007, when IGG Senior Branch members, together with members of CGI, formed the first all-female crew of the *Asgard* sail-training vessel. They successfully sailed the boat from Inverness to Howth.

On ending her term as chief commissioner in April 2007, Jillian van Turnhout noted in *Trefoil News*:

Over the past six years I have had my ups and downs as your chief commissioner. I have had so many happy moments filled with laughter and fun. On the other side I think it would be fair to say that at times it has been lonely and tough, or should I say challenging! Our membership numbers have continued to grow, both girls and

Disco revellers at Campa le Cheile.

adults. . . . We have embraced flexibility and adaptability in all areas of our programme. We have used our voice to speak on issues that affect girls and young women in Ireland. I could say a lot more but I think we are all part of an organisation of which we can be proud.

———◊———

Jillian was succeeded by Emer O'Sullivan, a long-time member of the IGG from Mayo, who noted on her election that 'as we move towards our centenary I would like to see the Irish Girl Guides grow from strength to strength. . . . I believe that, in order to continue to succeed as an organisation, we have to communicate effectively with one another. We have a great team in IGG and we need to work together as a team'.

Work was begun on updating the IGG website. The website had become overloaded with information: in order to continue to be at the cutting edge, the Irish Girl Guides needed a modern, easy-to-navigate website. Members were asked to complete an online survey about the site: over the following year and a half, a complete revamp of the website was undertaken, and in 2009 the new site was launched. Among other things, many valuable leader resources can now be accessed online. The Guide shop, which had been online for a few years, also got a new look, and its pages are now far easier to navigate. The IGG is continuing to keep up to date with its publications and PR material, and it is often easier to

Members of IGG and CGI on the bowsprit of Asgard II.

Opposite: *Members of IGG and CGI on the yards of Asgard II.*

reissue these online. The website has a more modern look for ease of use for parents, members and prospective new members. Many units, districts, areas and regions also have a web presence, with many starting websites or having a strong presence on the social-networking site Facebook.

Even the badges are more modern. No longer are they 'proficiency badges' but rather 'interest badges'. While many of the traditional badges, such as Book Lover/Reader, Knotter and Cook have been updated, there are also new badges available. For the Brownies, there are badges on Discovering Faith, Cultural Diversity, Foreign Language and Disability Awareness, and for the Guides on Chocolate, Film Lover, Beautician, Renewable Energy, Ski-ing and Team Player. In all aspects of its programme, Guiding also seeks to remain relevant to the children in the organisation.

An outreach resource pack was launched in 2008 by Barry Andrews TD, the Minister for Children and Youth Affairs. The pack challenges all leaders to reflect on perceptions and practices in relation to working with girls and young women on identity and minority issues. The Irish Girl Guides wanted their membership to reflect the population in Ireland today, so that various minority groups in each local community would be mirrored in the membership of the nearest IGG unit. Inclusion has been important from the very beginning of the movement. The Guide and Scout movements had been set up by the Baden-Powells as youth organisations. They wanted the movement to be

South West Region Gold Award Guides show off their impressive display of badges.

all-inclusive and to offer opportunities for girls and boys to mix with children of every faith, creed and colour. This has been a central tenet of Guiding and Scouting, and the IGG has always sought to promote diversity within its ranks. As part of the outreach programme, a Guide unit was started in Our Lady's Hospital for Sick Children in Crumlin: a team of volunteers run Guide meetings on a rota basis to ensure that patients who would like to be IGG members while they are in hospital can do so. Numbers are small, and ability varies from week to week, so it is an interesting challenge for all those who volunteer.

Barry Andrews TD launching the IGG Outreach Resource Pack, 2008.

Elspeth Henderson ended her term as chairman of the world board at the WAGGGS world conference in South Africa in 2008. At the conference, she was awarded the WAGGGS Silver Medal, the organisation's highest honour. Elspeth was presented with it for her dedication to the world association for more than three decades. Elspeth is one of only five people who have received the medal since it was introduced in 1992.

On 6 December 2008, a national event, Power Day, was held in Newbridge in conjunction with the National Youth Council of Ireland, the Irish Astronomical Society, and Friends of Londiani, who ran a number of the sessions. Girls from many parts of the country travelled to Newbridge for a day of fun, learning and activity. Each girl attended a session on the Promise, the Millennium Development Goals (MDGs) and Dance. They looked at what the Promise meant

*Elspeth Henderson,
chairman of the
World Board
receiving her
WAGGGS Silver
Medal.*

to them, and what the MDGs were, how they came about, and what they felt needed to happen in order to achieve them. Leaders were also busy throughout the day taking part in similar activities to those being followed by the girls, albeit done from the adult-leaders' perspective. Leaders completed sessions on MDGs and the Promise, contagious diseases, maternal health, development education and either One World Week or outreach activities.

Child welfare and safety has always been core to the Guide ethos, and in 2009 an 'Irish Girl Guides Code of Ethics' training module was launched. This training includes a code-of-behaviour module, which is an integral part of providing a safe environment for children and young people, as well as those who work with them. It also delivers a comprehensive awareness and training in child protection. The training provides leaders with an understanding of the relevance of child protection to Guiding, and how to respond to and report disclosures, concerns or suspicions in relation to child abuse.

Ladybirds celebrated their twentieth birthday in 2009. There were parties all over the country at unit, district and area level, with face painting and magicians. Practically every Ladybird in the country celebrated the birthday in some way. A DVD was also issued.

Recruitment and retention of leaders continues to be a constant challenge for the Irish Girl Guides; new and innovative ideas to combat this problem are continually being explored. During 2009, a membership ad hoc committee was set up. The committee has been looking at why girls leave the association at a certain age and how best to increase membership. Membership numbers have always been an issue for Guides and Scouts worldwide. Even Lord Baden-Powell commented on it, when he said: 'It would be an interesting study to find out why each boy who is a Scout first joins the Scouts. It would also be interesting to ascertain why each ex-Scout left the Scouts.'

During 2009, outreach taster days were held to promote Guiding in areas where numbers were flagging. A team of dedicated leaders led by the outreach development officer, Catherine O'Connor, travelled the country running free workshops. These workshops gave girls in the community the opportunity to try out some Guiding activities, such as games, team challenges, arts and crafts, and songs. Their favourite activities included parachute games for Ladybirds, egg drop and mini-Olympics for Brownies, and throw the ball, outdoor cooking and blindfolded maze for Guides.

The IGG logo of the traditional trefoil and Celtic knot had been introduced in 1938; it was felt that in 2010, as the association approached its centenary, it was time to modernise the IGG's image. A great deal of thought and work was put into the design of the new logo, and the executive committee considered many different options before making a decision. It was important to retain the Guiding trefoil, and the distinctive Irish Celtic knot remained part of the new design. The new logo was launched on 22 February 2010 and is now used on all Promise badges, uniforms, flags, stationery and promotional material.

As the logo was being updated, the opportunity was taken to consider updating all the branch uniforms. Since the existing red Ladybird and yellow Brownie

Ladybird Guides and their leaders celebrate twenty years of Ladybirds.

*Current and
prospective
members enjoying
activities at
Outreach Taster
Days, 2009.*

*New IGG logo,
February 2010.*

uniform tops were already in vibrant colours, it was decided to retain these and update the logo on them. Whereas the earlier uniforms had been based on navy and blue, with Guides, senior branch members and leaders all wearing similar navy tops, the new uniform features bright greens, pinks, lavenders and baby blues. Emer O'Sullivan, chief commissioner, recounts the decisions relating to the changes to the logo and uniform:

> We were very conscious when designing our new logo that we kept
> the traditional elements of Guiding: the trefoil, which is used by all

Guiding associations, together with the uniquely Irish Celtic knot, in a modern style. Up 'til now, our Guides and adult leaders all wore the same uniform. Our new range of uniforms has colours and styles to suit all ages. We now have a dynamic new image as we move into the next century of Guiding.

———◦∿∿◦———

Some of the biggest changes in the IGG happened in the ninety-ninth year of the organisation. The spirituality team, which had been formed in 2003, identified the need to review the Guide Promise. The Promise under review read:

> I promise on my honour to do my best to do my duty to God and my country, to help other people at all times and to obey the Guide Law.

New Ladybird Guide uniform.

New Senior Branch, Brownie Guide and Ladybird Guide uniforms.

Whatever their religion, ethnic group or background, all girls are welcomed into the sisterhood of Guiding, but as religious beliefs changed and Ireland opened up to new cultures and nationalities, it had to embrace new types of religion. Many leaders were looking for new ways of helping young people grow spiritually. In today's multicultural and ever-changing society, this is no easy task. One of the ways in which the Irish Girl Guides embraced this multiculturalism was by reviewing the Promise – for the first time since the 1930s.

All members were asked their thoughts on the Promise through discussion groups and a survey which was circulated at all regional conferences and inserted into *Trefoil News*. Members were asked if the words of the Promise needed to be altered slightly to be more inclusive, to better describe the life experience of the members, or even to make the Promise a more adequate expression of what is required of the girls in their society. The outcome of this process was an agreement that a slight alteration to the use of the word 'God' should be made to the Promise. On 18 April 2010, the Promise was officially changed to:

> I promise on my honour to do my best, to
> do my duty to my God† and my country,
> to help other people at all times and to
> obey the Guide Law.

† The word 'God' may be replaced by the word 'faith' according to one's spiritual beliefs.

*New Brownie
Guide uniform*

CONCLUSION

In a world fraught with uncertainty and fear, our movement
shines out as a golden chain against a dark background.

Lady Baden-Powell

The Girl Guide movement, which was started in Ireland in 1911, has all the same
fundamental principles, beliefs and aspirations one hundred years later. Guiding
has maintained its core ideology: all that has really changed is the uniforms. In
1911, it was not acceptable for girls to camp, run around, jump, be loud or, as it
was put at the time, act like boys. Guiding has done a lot to fight this stereotype,
and now, in a time when girls and boys are equal and have the same rights and
opportunities as each other, Guiding offers young women an opportunity to
develop to their fullest potential.

Over the past hundred years, Guiding in Ireland has developed and flourished
within a fast-changing society. It has survived emergencies and indeed thrived. At all
times, the Irish Girl Guides (in its various incarnations) has sought to work for the
good of its members. The IGG has moved with the times, engaged with national and
international socio-economic changes, embraced all relevant legislation, adapted its

*A Ranger renewing
her promise at Our
Chalet in
Switzerland 2009.*

uniform to account for taste, practicality and fashion, raised money for worthy causes, followed innovations in technology, and at all times maintained its core values (as expressed in the Promise and Law).

The Irish Girl Guides is also a strong and respected voice in European and international Guiding, with members representing the IGG at the highest levels of WAGGGS. The association has always encouraged its members to participate in international trainings and events, and Ireland can always be counted on to send a delegation to any event, in whatever part of the world it is being held.

The Irish Girl Guides, as a girl-only organisation, is distinctive. The organisation is youth-driven, dynamic and active. It offers a programme for girls and young women aged from five to twenty-six years of age. It is also open to volunteer leaders of all ages. Because of the all-female nature of the organisation, the girls are free to progress and express themselves in a comfortable setting. It is a space in which they can 'just be girls' without any pressure while learning the skills that will one day be invaluable to them in their personal, social and professional lives.

There is a strong emphasis on the outdoors, environment, community responsibility and teamwork. The girls' self-esteem and leadership skills are developed as they progress through Guiding. The IGG also actively promotes diversity and inclusion: girls and young women from all backgrounds and walks of life are part of the organisation.

There are Guides in twenty-five counties of Ireland (none in Leithrim); as of 2010, there were 10,471 members in the Republic of Ireland. Guiding continues to be a real and viable choice for young women, and many who join at the age of

five go on to become leaders or commissioners, or even to represent Ireland at European and international level.

The Irish Girl Guides is a member of a worldwide movement (WAGGGS) of over 10 million girls and young women in over 145 countries. As a result, there is a true awareness of global issues and sense of solidarity with their fellow Guides

National group selected to attend Wiltshire jubilee Camp, 1977.

around the globe. The girls learn all about campaigning and advocacy and there are also wonderful opportunities for travel and camps abroad for girls and leaders alike. Everyone has memories of camps and travel with Guiding, as life-changing experiences. The bonds and friendships made through Guiding are ones that survive for life.

The first hundred years of the Irish Girl Guides have been a thrilling adventure; as we celebrate the centenary of the IGG, we must not forget to look to the past. The IGG have much to celebrate, and it is important to remember those who began and carried on the adventure, and always to keep their spirit alive. Let's leave the final word to Lord Baden-Powell:

> So in our work indeed, in any work of life we should look forward, well forward, with high aims and hope; look around with joy and goodwill; look back with thankfulness at what has been accomplished and then press on with renewed vigour, with helpful initiative, and with broadened outlook, towards the highest goal, not forgetting to give a helping hand to others as we go. But when you look – look *wide*; and even when you think you are looking wide – look wider still.

Exploring the bog at Campa le Cheile.

A Ranger investiture in the 1920s.

Filling up the water supplies at Campa le Cheile.

OFFICE HOLDERS

Presidents

Mrs Katherine Guinness, 1960–64

Vacant, 1964–70

Miss Eileen O. Beatty, 1970–80

Mrs Frances Dwyer, 1980–87

Mrs Maimie Howie, 1987–95

Mrs Anne Bowen, 1995–2002

Ms Elspeth Henderson, 2002–2005

Mrs Dilys Lindsay, 2005–

Chief Commissioners

Viscountess Powerscourt, 1917–46

Viscountess Powerscourt, 1947–57

Miss Eileen O. Beatty, 1957–70

Mrs Frances Dwyer, 1970–76

Miss Marjorie Williams, 1976–81

Mrs Audrey Carr, 1981–90

Mrs Margaret Dunne, 1990–97

Mrs Hazel Convery, 1997–2001

Mrs Jillian van Turnhout, 2001–2007

Ms Emer O'Sullivan, 2007–

- behave responsibly in upholding the laws of the country

- be aware of and care for the needs of others

- appreciate and use environmental sources responsibly.

Members

Ladybird Guides are aged from five to seven years.

They follow a programme which is full of fun and helps them to:

- become more independent

- learn to care and share

- discover the world around them

- learn about the family of Guiding to which they belong

- take part in activities, including songs and games.

The Ladybird Guide Promise: I will try to do my best to love my God† and help other people.

† The word 'God' may be replaced by the word 'faith' according to one's spiritual beliefs.

Ladybird Guide Motto: Ladybird Guides care and share.

Brownie Guides are aged from six and a half to eleven years. They follow a programme full of interest, fun and variety which:

- encourages self-development and thoughtfulness towards others

- introduces them to the international family of Guiding

- teaches them respect for cultures and religions different from their own

- develops teamwork and sharing.

APPENDIX

The Irish Girl Guides
Some Facts

Mission Statement

The mission of the Irish Girl Guides is to enable girls and young women to develop to their fullest potential as responsible citizens of the world.

Aims and Objectives

The Irish Girl Guides provides an environment where girls and young women from all backgrounds can grow in self-confidence and develop a variety of skills in an unpressurised atmosphere. Through a variety of activities, girls and young women are encouraged to:

- develop leadership skills

- develop a knowledge and understanding of spiritual values in their daily lives

- be involved in decision-making

- earn practical indoor and outdoor skills

- participate in the international aspects of Guiding

Brownie Guide Promise: I promise to do my best, to do my duty to my God †
and my country. To help those at home every day and to obey the Brownie
Guide law.

† The word 'God' may be replaced by the word 'faith' according to one's spiritual beliefs.

Brownies Guide Law: A Brownie thinks of others before herself, and does
a Good Turn every day.

Brownie Guide Motto: Lend a hand.

Guides are aged from ten and a half to fifteen years. They follow a programme of
challenges which equips them to:

- have fun through adventure

- offer voluntary service to Guiding and the community

- enjoy the out-of-doors

- learn practical skills

- participate in the international aspect of Guiding

- develop their own spirituality and respect other cultures and religions.

Guide Laws:

1   A Guide is honest and reliable.

2   A Guide is loyal.

3   A Guide is useful and helps others.

4   A Guide is a friend to all and a sister to every other Guide.

5   A Guide is polite and considerate.

6   A Guide cares for all living things and their environment.

7   A Guide is responsible and respects authority.

8   A Guide has courage and is cheerful in difficulties.

9   A Guide makes good use of time, talents and materials.

10   A Guide respects herself and others in all she thinks, says and does.

Guide Promise: I promise on my honour to do my best, to do my duty, to my God†
and my country, to help other people at all times and to obey the Guide laws.
†The word 'God' may be replaced by the word 'faith' according to one's spiritual beliefs.

Guide Motto: Be prepared.

Ranger Guides are aged from fourteen and a half to twenty-one years. The
programme for the girls' self-development is based on:

■ fun and adventure service to the community

■ outdoor activities

■ international opportunities

■ spirituality

■ craftwork.

Special Responsibility: My special responsibility as a Ranger Guide is to render
service by taking this Promise out into the wider world.

Flexibility within the programme is of prime importance, and the girls set their
own pace and syllabus within the unit.

Young Leaders are aged from fifteen to eighteen years. Leadership skills are developed through working with Ladybird, Brownie and Guide units, thus helping the girls to grow in self-confidence to become the leaders of tomorrow.

Special Commitment: My special commitment as a Young Leader is to practise the Guide Law and Promise in my daily life and to grow in the skills and responsibilities of Leadership.

Adult Leaders are over eighteen years of age. They have an interest and enthusiasm in working with young people and are prepared to give some time on a regular basis. Training is provided in:

- leadership skills/confidence-building

- programme ideas

- environmental issues

- international opportunities

- psychology of the child

- values of Guiding.

Leadership is voluntary, rewarding, challenging, fun, and a way of making new friends.

Trefoil Guild is made up of former members of the Irish Girl Guides who have given up active Guiding but want to enjoy the fun and fellowship of the Guide movement. Each Guild has its own programme of activities, and members retain their links with international and local Guiding.

International visitors from Canada at Campa le Cheile.

GUIDING GLOSSARY

adalia   a name used for a Ladybird leader

badge tab   a piece of navy material worn by leaders to hold pin badges

branch weekend   an annual training weekend for leaders at which each leader
receives branch-specific training

branches   the different age groups that the Irish Girl Guides work with

brown owl   a name used for a Brownie Guide leader

Brownie Guide   a member of the IGG aged six and a half to eleven years

camp   a holiday under canvas

captain   a name used for a Guide leader

coccinella   a name used for a Ladybird leader

collective emblems   a badge which can be awarded to a Brownie Guide or Guide
after she has completed a particular group of interest badges

colour party   the group of two or three people responsible for carrying, raising
and lowering the flag

colours flag

commissioner a warranted leader with a specific responsibility, e.g. district, international

commissioning a ceremony where a Young Leader makes her Promise with the special Young Leader commitment and receives a Young Leader Trefoil pin

company a name often used for a Guide unit

core challenges the compulsory sections of the Brownie Guide and Guide programmes

distribution centre place where uniforms, badges and resources for leaders may be purchased

drill a marching ceremony for Guides

enrolment when a member makes her Promise and is presented with the appropriate branch trefoil pin

event pack the necessary forms for running an overnight event, and useful charts and checklists

executive committee the national committee responsible for the management of the Irish Girl Guides

garden/square the shape the Ladybirds stand in for ceremonies good turn helping someone without being asked or paid

Guide   a member of the IGG aged ten and a half to fifteen years Guide
sign a symbol of Guiding throughout the world

Guider   a leader with the Irish Girl Guides

horseshoe   the shape the Guides stand in for ceremonies

indoor licence advisor   an experienced leader willing to and capable of sharing
her knowledge of indoor activities

interest badges   badge syllabi that the girls can complete on various topics, to
match their interests

investiture   a ceremony where a Ranger Guide makes her Promise with the
special   Ranger commitment and receives a Ranger trefoil pin

kit list   a list of the clothing, equipment, etc needed for an event

Ladybird day out   an annual day out for Ladybird Guides

Ladybird Guide   a member of the IGG aged five to seven years

leader   an adult leader who works with a unit

link badges and certificates   for Ladybird Guides going to Brownie Guides, or
for Brownie Guides going to Guides

log book   a copy or similar book for recording events, e.g. accident log book

logo   the IGG emblem adapted for each branch

membership fee   the annual subscription to the Irish Girl Guides

national standing committees   national committees with specific areas of responsibility, e.g. Brownie Guide branch committee, adult training and outdoors committee

neckerchief   a triangular scarf worn around the neck

numbered challenges   the 'pick and choose' section of the Brownie programme. A numbered challenge pack with resources for these activities is available.

optional challenges   the 'pick and choose' section of the Guide programme. An optional challenge pack with resources for these activities is available.

outdoor advisor an experienced leader who is willing to and capable of sharing her knowledge on outdoor and indoor activities

pack a name often used for a Brownie Guide unit

pack holiday   an event for Brownie Guides involving at least one overnight away from home

powwow   when Brownie Guides sit in a circle with their leaders for a discussion

programme   the totality of activities and experiences provided for members

programme and training committee   the national committee responsible for coordinating the development and delivery of all aspects of the Guiding programme

Rainbow   a name used for a Ladybird leader

Ranger Guide   a member of the IGG aged fourteen and a half to twenty-one years

regional committee member   a member of the regional committee and a representative of that region on a national standing committee

regional development officer   an employee of the IGG whose responsibility is to help develop Guiding in her region, in conjunction with the leaders

regional teams   a group of leaders in a region with a designated focus, e.g. regiona Guide team, regional outdoor team

resource centres   a support facility in some areas or regions

revels   a day of fun activities held for Brownie Guides

roll books   a record of attendance at meetings and events

safety guidelines   a booklet containing important information on insurance, safety and activities

Sash   a band of material worn by Brownie Guides and Guides onto which they sew their badges

senior branch   members of the IGG from fourteen and a half to twenty-six years of age

Snowy Owl   a name used for a Brownie Guide leader

special-issue badges   badges which a unit can opt to do, focused on a particular issue, e.g. drug awareness, outdoors, celebrations

square/garden   the shape the Ladybirds stand in for ceremonies

Oppoite: *Camp Conway.*

subscriptions   the contribution to the running of the unit, paid weekly, monthly or annually depending on the unit

Tawny Owl   a name used for a Brownie Guide leader

term of office   the length of time a member can hold a particular position

The Welly   the Senior Branch magazine of the IGG

trefoil   a three-part emblem, representing the three parts of the Promise

Trefoil Guild   a non-uniformed group of women who make the Promise and remain linked with Guiding

Trefoil House   the building shared by National Office and the Dublin Distribution Centre

Trefoil News   the leaders' magazine of the Irish Girl Guides

unit   a group of members with leaders, registered by the local commissioner at National Office

unit helper   an interested adult who does not wish to or cannot (e.g. a father) become a warranted leader

warrant   the Irish Girl Guides licence issued to a leader

woggle   a woven leather band worn around the neckerchief

young Guider   a leader aged up to twenty-six years

Young Leader   a member of the IGG aged fifteen to eighteen years working with a unit

Senior Branch and Guides modelling the new uniform in 2010.